PLOTINUS

PLOTINUS

An Introduction to the *Enneads*

DOMINIC J. O'MEARA

CLARENDON PRESS · OXFORD
1993

Oxford University Press, Walton Street, Oxford OX2 6DP
Oxford New York Toronto
Delhi Bombay Calcutta Madras Karachi
Kuala Lumpur Singapore Hong Kong Tokyo
Nairobi Dar es Salaam Cape Town
Melbourne Auckland Madrid
and associated companies in
Berlin Ibadan

Oxford is a trade mark of Oxford University Press

Published in the United States
by Oxford University Press Inc., New York

British Library Cataloguing in Publication Data
Data available

Library of Congress Cataloging in Publication Data
O'Meara, Dominic J.
Plotinus: an introduction to the Enneads / Dominic J. O'Meara.
p. cm.
Includes bibliographical references and indexes.
1. Plotinus. Enneads. 2. Philosophy. I. Title.
B693.E6048 1993 186'.4—dc20 92-24776
ISBN 0–19–875121–4

Typeset by Pentacor PLC, High Wycombe, Bucks
Printed and bound in Great Britain
on acid-free paper by
Biddles Ltd,
Guildford and King's Lynn

For Carra

Preface

This book is intended to be of service to the reader who, if not unfamiliar with ancient Greek philosophy, does not know Plotinus at first hand and would like to read his work. Today many paths lead back to Plotinus. Our increasing interest in late antiquity, a period of history of great importance for Western culture, brings us to the philosophers who made a major creative contribution to the period, Plotinus and his successors (they are labelled today collectively as 'Neoplatonists'). The historian of philosophy is more aware than ever before that the Neoplatonists shaped ancient philosophy as it was transmitted to (and established) philosophy in the Islamic and Byzantine worlds and in the West of the Middle Ages, the Renaissance, and the Enlightenment. The history of theology, literature, and art in the same periods and places is also marked by Plotinus' ideas.[1] Finally modern philosophers' interests have changed to the point where they no longer hesitate to look beyond the traditional sources of inspiration in antiquity that are Plato and Aristotle. Our improved understanding of Plotinus shows him to be a far more challenging philosopher than would have been suspected a few generations ago.

The most important event in the progress of modern work on Plotinus was the publication of the first scientific edition of his works by Paul Henry and Hans-Rudolph Schwyzer in 1951–73. Essential research was also done during this time (mostly in France and Germany) on Plotinus' philosophical background. In the English-speaking world serious work on Plotinus was pioneered by A. Hilary Armstrong, whose translation (1966–88), accompanied by the Henry–Schwyzer edition (slightly revised), has at last made available a complete, reliable, and clear English version of Plotinus. Excellent

---

[1] For more details see below, Epilogue.

systematic accounts and analytical discussions of Plotinus are also available now in English.[2] However the reader, despite this major progress, may still find Plotinus' writings difficult of access. In this book I try to make the first approach to the texts less daunting.

For reasons given below in the Introduction I have taken in the following chapters a number of philosophical questions (often traditional in Greek philosophy) and attempt to show how Plotinus, in selected treatises, discusses these questions in relation to the views of his predecessors and argues for his own position. My hope is that this approach will bring the reader nearer to the actual text of Plotinus' treatises while giving some idea of the thinking that led Plotinus to elaborate his philosophy. I have arranged the chapters in such a way that the later chapters presuppose ideas first introduced in the earlier chapters. Thus the sequence of chapters is conceived more as a way of preparing the approach of the reader to Plotinus than as representing some order in Plotinus' works or world. Wherever possible I quote passages from Plotinus, in my translation, inserting in square brackets information needed for a better understanding of these passages. By using terminology close to that adopted by Armstrong, I hope to facilitate the use of this book in conjunction with his translation.

My colleagues in the field may find that some matters are oversimplified here or even omitted; in my defence I can only remind them of the purpose of the book, which is not intended as a contribution to specialized research. However I have tried sometimes to convey an impression of the problems that arise when one looks at Plotinus more closely.[3] If anything the uninitiated reader might sometimes feel that parts of the book are rather complicated and abstract. It is difficult to see how this can be entirely avoided without giving a misleading idea of the philosopher.

A sabbatical grant from the University of Fribourg made completion of this book possible. For very helpful, detailed, and often stimulating comments I am greatly indebted to A. H.

---

[2] See 'Guide to Further Reading', preliminary section.

[3] In general I have avoided the use of scholarly annotation. The reader will find in the 'Guide to Further Reading' (below) additional references to Plotinian texts and indications concerning modern discussion of the texts.

Armstrong, E. Emilsson, J. O'Meara, and Oxford University Press's reader.

D.J.O'M.

Fribourg, Switzerland
October 1991

Contents

Introduction
Plotinus' Life and Works

We depend for practically all of what we know about Plotinus' life and works on the labours of one of his pupils, Porphyry. Porphyry's *Life of Plotinus* (or *Vita Plotini*), one of the most interesting of ancient biographies to survive, is the principal source of information about Plotinus' life. Porphyry placed it at the beginning of his edition of Plotinus' works and it is this edition (the *Enneads*) which prevailed in antiquity and which we have inherited. Porphyry published the *Life* and *Enneads* at the beginning of the fourth century AD, some thirty years after Plotinus' death. He was already 30 years of age and highly educated in literature and philosophy when he became a member of Plotinus' circle in Rome in 263. His devotion to Plotinus, then and after, did not exclude his having his own interests. These interests shape his biography and edition of Plotinus, defining how we should read the life and writings of his master. We would do well then to take account of the point of view of our guide as he gives us access to the exceptional person and philosopher whom he felt so privileged to know.

1. Plotinus' Life

One of Porphyry's aims in writing the *Life of Plotinus* is to show that he had been entrusted by the master with the task of editing his works (*Life*, chs. 7, 24). Other pupils had prepared editions of various sorts, Amelius (100 volumes of notes!) and Eustochius. But Porphyry wishes to impose his edition as the 'authorized' version. He also sees himself as the focus around which revolved the actual writing of the works. The twenty-one treatises Plotinus composed between 254 and 263 (i.e. before Porphyry's arrival) are, Porphyry suggests, immature, whereas those written after Porphyry's departure from Rome in 269 show decline (*Life*, 6. 28–37). While this piece of self-glorification on Porphyry's part is absurd—Plotinus was not an immature youth but in his fifties in 254–63 and the works he composed after Porphyry's departure are far from showing decline—it does seem likely that Porphyry, being more of a literary man than Plotinus, encouraged his master to write more. And indeed the treatises written in and after 263 (e.g. *Ennead* VI. 4–5) show great freedom and depth as compared with the rather stiff and didactic pieces that Plotinus had written before.

Porphyry has another purpose in the *Life*: to prepare the reader for approaching Plotinus' treatises. He does this, not only by providing useful background information about Plotinus and his works, but also by portraying Plotinus as the ideal philosopher. This portrait is intended to inspire and guide us as we begin our reading of the *Enneads*, as we take, that is, our first steps toward wisdom. The ideal is Porphyry's, not Plotinus'. This creates a revealing tension between the facts about Plotinus reported by Porphyry and the ideal that Porphyry wants these facts to exemplify. We might consider the following cases.

The *Life* begins as follows: 'Plotinus, the philosopher who was our contemporary, seemed to be ashamed that he was in the body. It is because of this attitude that he could not bear to speak about his race, his parents, and his native land.' To grasp what is at stake here we should notice that, according to ancient literary theory, Porphyry ought to have begun the description of his hero by dealing with the hero's race, parents, and native land. Porphyry knew this, but his ambitions as biographer were frustrated by Plotinus' silence. Already at the start the biographer's intentions are at odds with his subject's attitudes. How account for Plotinus' silence? Porphyry finds a philosophical explanation: it was because Plotinus seemed to be ashamed that he was in the body. However, shame is not an attitude to the body characteristic of Plotinus (see below Ch. 8 s. 4, Ch. 9).

The tension between the biographer and his subject can also be felt when Porphyry seeks to invest his ideal philosopher with divine powers, divine inspiration, and a quasi-religious, magical aura. He reports that a certain Olympius of Alexandria in Egypt, having attempted to use magic against Plotinus, asserted that the power of Plotinus' soul was so great that the attack was repelled. When an Egyptian priest evoked Plotinus' guardian spirit in the temple of Isis in Rome, it turned out to be no mere spirit but a god (ch. 10)! This image of Plotinus is given divine confirmation by the oracle of Apollo obtained after Plotinus' death by Amelius (ch. 22).

What are we to make of all this? Who are Porphyry's sources for the story about Olympius and for the episode in the temple of Isis? What could Plotinus do about an oracle conferred on him after he was dead? Both Amelius and Porphyry were very much taken with religious movements, ritual, and oracles of all sorts. Plotinus did not share these interests:

Amelius became keen on sacrificial rites and went out doing the rounds of the temples at the New Moon and the religious feasts. He once wanted to take Plotinus with him, but Plotinus said, 'they [the gods] should come to me, not I to them'. We were not able to understand what he might have meant with such grand words and we did not dare to ask him. (*Life*, 10. 33–8)

Although Amelius and Porphyry were among Plotinus' most dedicated and closest pupils, we should not assume that they always represented the views of their teacher. In the present instance it is clear that neither Amelius nor Porphyry understood Plotinus' attitude to religion and its rites. We must bear this in mind as we read what Porphyry tells us in the *Life*.

Let us turn to some of the biographical facts given by the *Life*. Porphyry tells us that Plotinus died at the age of 66 in 270, which gives an approximate birth date of 204. He reports that Plotinus took up the study of philosophy at the age of 28 in Alexandria in Egypt. He was inspired by one teacher in particular, Ammonius Sakkas (about whom we know very little), and stayed with him for eleven years (ch. 3). He then joined the military expedition under the Emperor Gordian III against the Persians (242). (Porphyry says that he wanted to become acquainted with Persian and Indian wisdom, but this is a standard motif in ancient biographies of sages.) In the course of the expedition the emperor was murdered by his own soldiers (244). Plotinus escaped to Antioch and went on to Rome where he settled.

These facts can be fleshed out in various ways. It is not unlikely that Plotinus was an Egyptian of strong Hellenic culture. As a young man in Alexandria and later throughout his life in Rome Plotinus found himself in a world that went from one profound crisis to another. The great age of the Roman Empire, an age of political stability, military security, and economic and social development, had ended with the Severan dynasty (193–235). Plotinus witnessed a succession of emperors whose reigns, usually a matter of months, routinely ended in assassination: the murder of Gordian III is one in a long series. Continuing civil war accompanied unrelenting and frequently catastrophic invasions of the empire from Persia and Northern Europe. This brought serious damage to agriculture, food shortages, frequent epidemics, depopulation, interruption of trade, serious inflation, heavy taxation, increasing militarization of the administration. Such was the psychological stress that all of this brought that we can speak with E. R. Dodds of this period as an 'age of anxiety'.

Plotinus' participation in the expedition against the Persians is very curious. What were his functions? He was hardly a soldier or a gentleman volunteer such as another philosopher, Descartes, would later be. Perhaps Plotinus acted as a court philosopher of the sort Roman emperors sometimes liked to have in their entourage. This suggests that the contacts Plotinus would later have in Rome with members of the ruling class go back to his earlier years in Egypt.

Returning to Porphyry's *Life*, we find Plotinus beginning to teach in Rome to a circle of friends and pupils. (He occupied no formal teaching post.) He lived in the house of Gemina, presumably a rich patroness. His circle included senators and other politicians, doctors, literary men, a number of women, all coming from different backgrounds, Egyptian, Syrian, Arabian, as well as Italian and Roman. An inner circle of pupils collaborated closely in the work of the group. It included Amelius and Porphyry. Plotinus' links with

Roman power developed into a friendship with the Emperor Gallienus (253–68) and his wife. Plotinus tried to use this occasion to found a city in Campania, to be called Platonopolis and to be governed, it seems, according to Plato's political ideas. However the project met opposition in Court and was not realized. Plotinus seems to have had good practical sense: he was sought after as a guardian for the children of deceased friends and was a successful arbitrator of disputes (ch. 9).

The main activity of Plotinus' circle was philosophical discussion. (What Plotinus himself hoped to achieve with this is described below in Chapter 10.) The sessions were open to all. Amelius gave Porphyry an account of the earlier years of teaching in Rome: 'The sessions, Amelius told me, were confused and much nonsense was spoken since he [Plotinus] stimulated enquiry among the participants' (*Life*, ch. 3). Porphyry tells us what he found when he joined the group in 263. The sessions of the group might begin with a pupil reading from a fairly recent work (it might be a commentary on Plato or on Aristotle) by a Platonist such as Numenius or Atticus or by an Aristotelian philosopher such as Alexander of Aphrodisias. Plotinus would then comment, not following the text word by word, but taking an individual and different line, using the approach of his teacher Ammonius (ch. 14). This seems to have involved the selective interpretation of a passage, particularly in Plato, and discussion of the philosophical problem it raised. Much time was spent in debates (hardly more disciplined than those earlier sessions of which Amelius complained) in which Plotinus made no attempt to impose his views: 'His teaching seemed like a conversation and he did not reveal immediately to anyone the logical necessities contained in what he said' (ch. 18). Porphyry then gives an example of an occasion when it took some time for him to grasp and accept Plotinus' position. Another debate is described in ch. 13:

For three days I, Porphyry, asked him how soul is with the body and he persisted in his explanation. A certain Thaumasius came in and said that he wanted to hear an overall treatment to be put in books and that he could not bear Porphyry's answers and questions. But Plotinus said, 'But if we do not solve the difficulties raised by Porphyry's questions, we will not be able to say anything to be put in a book.'

In this chapter Porphyry brings us very near to seeing Plotinus the man: 'When he spoke his intellect illuminated even his face. Of pleasing aspect, he was then even more beautiful to see. Sweating slightly, his gentleness showed as did his kindness while being questioned and his rigour.'

From Porphyry's invaluable descriptions of such sessions, it emerges that they concerned sometimes the correct interpretation of a passage in Plato, sometimes the resolution of a philosophical problem such as that of the relation between soul and body. In fact these two aspects are closely related. Plotinus saw in Plato the philosopher who had come nearest to the truth. Interpreting Plato correctly would involve finding the right solution to the problem at issue (the passage in Plato might for instance have to do with soul and body). As Plato's dialogues allow for many different interpretations, Plotinus would take account of these interpretations as representing possible philosophical answers, to be accepted or rejected. And as other philosophers such as Aristotle and the Presocratics had insight, they too would sometimes require interpretation. The modern historian would object to Plotinus' approach: the method for reaching a correct (historical) interpretation of a text in Plato is quite different from the analysis of a philosophical problem; what is a true reading of what Plato says, for example, about the universe is not necessarily true of the universe itself. However, Plotinus was a philosopher, not an historian or literary exegete.

In the *Life* (ch. 14) Porphyry gives us a list of the commentators on Plato and on Aristotle read in Plotinus' school: Severus, Cronius, Numenius, Gaius, Atticus (the Platonists), Aspasius, Alexander of Aphrodisias, Adrastus (the Aristotelians), and others. We know very little about some of these philosophers and for the rest we are obliged to find out what we can from the fragments or (at best) portions of their work that have survived. Dating from the first two centuries AD they were teachers who, like Plotinus, found in Plato or Aristotle an ancient repository of truth the interpretation of which would give philosophical answers. The Platonists (called 'Middle Platonists' by modern historians, to distinguish them from the members of Plato's own school and from the 'Neoplatonists', Plotinus and his successors) attempted to elaborate systems of Platonic philosophy on the basis of interpretation of Plato's dialogues read sometimes in the light of Aristotelian or Stoic ideas. The results they reached differed enough to give Plotinus a wide range of options. In the following chapters I shall refer to the views of the Platonists best known to us, Numenius and Atticus, as well as to the work of a Platonist not named by Porphyry, the *Didaskalikos* of Alcinous,[1] since it is one of the rare texts of Platonic philosophy to survive from the second century. The Aristotelians Aspasius and Alexander saw in Aristotle what the Platonists saw in Plato: they too worked towards elaborating a systematic philosophy on the basis of interpreting Aristotle. Fortunately large portions of Alexander's work survive. As his ideas had a considerable impact on Plotinus, I shall introduce them also in the following chapters.

Porphyry indicates that Plotinus' interpretation of Plato was hardly orthodox. It was not accepted by Porphyry's former teacher in Athens, Longinus, and was attacked by some unnamed critics in Greece who accused Plotinus of plagiarizing Numenius (ch. 17). Plotinus set his closest pupils to respond to these criticisms. A more serious threat was the influence exerted on some members of his circle by a religious movement known as 'Gnosticism' in modern scholarship. It will be necessary later in the book to say more about this movement, which might be sketched briefly as follows.

Of bewildering diversity and complexity, Gnosticism was a religious movement which usually took the form of a Christian heresy. Spreading throughout the Roman Empire in the first centuries AD, it promised salvation to the privileged few who were in possession of a special revelation or knowledge (*gnosis*). This knowledge declared the world in which we live to be the handiwork of evil and ignorant forces, a world in which fragments of a higher world, a world of good divinities, are imprisoned. As these divine elements plunged in the body we await liberation from our body and the powers of evil. Very many variations and complications of this

---

[1] Modern scholars have until recently been in the habit of referring to this author (incorrectly) as Albinus.

general scheme can be found in Gnosticism, as is made clear by the hostile reports of Church writers and by the few authentic Gnostic documents that have come down to us. The latter include notably a collection of Gnostic books dating from the fourth century discovered in the 1940s near Nag Hammadi in Egypt. This collection contains versions of texts actually named by Porphyry in the *Life* (ch. 16) and thus allows us to read some of the kind of writing whose influence Plotinus felt to be so pernicious.

Whereas the Christian enemies of Gnosticism considered it to be a heresy generated in part by the corrupting power of Greek philosophy, Plotinus thought of it as an arrogant and perverse reading of Plato. Its influence was serious enough to require Plotinus' direct attention in a number of his treatises. He also got his pupils to write critiques of Gnosticism (*Life*, ch. 16). It is possible (but not certain) that he criticized Christianity, with which he could hardly have had much sympathy. Certainly Porphyry published at some point in his life a very important attack on the Christian religion.

The Emperor Gallienus was murdered in 268 and the general anarchy (which had not abated in his reign) continued. In the last two years of his life Plotinus wrote more about moral issues: evil, providence, happiness. In 269, suffering from a serious depression, Porphyry left Rome on his master's advice, going to Sicily. Plotinus fell ill and his circle appears to have started to disperse. Dying of a disease that we cannot now identify with accuracy (possibly tuberculosis or a form of leprosy) Plotinus retired to the country house of a deceased friend and pupil near Minturno in Campania. Attended by another pupil, the doctor Eustochius, he died in 270. Eustochius reported to the absent Porphyry that Plotinus' last words were: 'Try to lead the god in you up to the divine in the universe' (*Life*, 2. 26–7).

2. Plotinus' Works

Inspired by the portrait of Plotinus as the ideal sage, the reader of the *Life* is intended to move on to what follows, to begin reading

Plotinus' works as edited by Porphyry, the *Enneads*. Here also Porphyry guides us, by means of the way in which he organized the edition. Fortunately he explains his editorial procedures in the *Life*. He first cut up some of Plotinus' treatises so as to increase their number to fifty-four. The purpose of this was to have a number that is the product of the perfect number 6 (6 is both $1 + 2 + 3$ and $1 \times 2 \times 3$) and of the number 9, symbol of totality as the last of first numbers (from 1 to 10). This cutting-up of treatises is not on the whole too misleading, as the various parts of the divided treatises usually follow each other in the edition (VI. 1, VI. 2, and VI. 3, for example). However, one major treatise suffered badly from this treatment, as we will see shortly.

Porphyry's next operation was to arrange the fifty-four treatises into six sets of nine treatises, 'nines' (*enneades* in Greek), assigning the treatises to various sets depending on what he considered their main theme to be. The thematic grouping was intended to lay out a path for the ascent of the soul of the reader, going from the first steps to the ultimate goal of Plotinian philosophy. Thus the first set of nine treatises (*Enn*. I. 1–9) concerns moral questions, the second and third sets (*Enn*. II. 1–9 and III. 1–9) discuss the natural world, the fourth (*Enn*. IV. 1–9) deals with soul, the fifth (*Enn*. V. 1–9) with intellect, and the sixth (*Enn*. VI. 1–9) with the One.

This arrangement brings serious disadvantages with it. First, Plotinus writes more like Plato than like Aristotle in the sense that he does not confine himself in one work to covering a particular subject or field. His treatises often deal with many different matters and thus do not lend themselves easily to a thematic grouping. Second, one of the major treatises, that directed against Gnosticism, was divided by Porphyry into four pieces, the pieces being assigned to different sets. They are III. 8, V. 8, V. 5, II. 9. What makes it possible to see that these severed members, scattered throughout the compartments of Porphyry's edition, originally belonged together is the fact that Porphyry also tells us in what chronological order the treatises were composed. According to this chronological order (*Life*, chs. 4–6), the texts in question are numbers 30 to 33.

Porphyry's final editorial intervention was to insert titles (some of his own making, some current in the school) for the treatises, as

Plotinus showed no interest in this (or in any other) convention in publishing (*Life*, 4. 16–18, 8. 1–7). Apart from the possible addition of a few explanatory phrases, Porphyry did not seriously interfere, it appears, with the actual text of Plotinus' treatises and for this we must be grateful. Plotinus' style is so individual and free that modern scholars have had to learn to resist the temptation to standardize or 'correct' his writing.

The conclusion one may draw so far is that Porphyry's arrangement of Plotinus' works is wholly artificial and sometimes misleading. It has nothing to recommend it, apart from offering us a rather esoteric way of referring to Plotinus' treatises.[2] If we do not follow Porphyry's editorial guidance, how then should we approach Plotinus? Two questions need to be considered: how individual treatises might be approached, and in what order the treatises should be read.

Porphyry indicates twice (*Life*, chs. 4, 5) that treatises originated in discussions that took place in Plotinus' school. The incident with Thaumasius mentioned above shows that Plotinus would not write down his thoughts until problems had been thoroughly debated in the school. The various opinions of the philosophers (Plato, of course, but also Aristotle and the Stoics) and the positions of the more recent commentators on Plato and Aristotle would be considered. Plotinus would also take account of the various views of his pupils before formulating his position. In view of this it seems to be preferable to read the treatises as relating to debates involving the exegesis of a text in Plato or the solution of a problem, debates which evolved in the context provided by the opinions of Plotinus' immediate philosophical predecessors.[3] I shall adopt this approach

---

[2] The standard way of referring to Plotinus' works is to give the number in Porphyry's edition (e.g. set number III, treatise number 8 = *Ennead* III. 8) followed by the number according to the chronological order given in square brackets (thus: III. 8 [30]) and the chapter and line numbers (thus: *Ennead* III. 8 [30]. 1. 1–2). The division into chapters was introduced by Marsilio Ficino in his Latin translation of Plotinus (Florence, 1492). Materials missing from Ficino's version of *Ennead* IV. 7, ch. 8, were subsequently numbered as chapters 8^1–8^5.

[3] For Plotinus' statement of his method see *Enn.* III. 7 [45]. 1. 7–17. Plotinus did not write the treatises simply in order to record such debates. His usual purpose in writing (as in teaching) was to lead us through philosophy to the Good (see below, Ch. 10).

in the following chapters, taking as starting-points various philosophical problems (and the relevant texts in Plato), showing how, in certain treatises, Plotinus formulates his views in the light of a critique of the options found in the work of his predecessors. It is my purpose by this means to bring the reader closer to the actual workings of the treatises and to convey some idea of how Plotinus' philosophy evolved.

As regards the order in which to read the treatises, if one intends to read them all, it would be preferable to follow the chronological order of composition (see above). This allows one to read the divided treatises as wholes and to see how Plotinus takes up and develops points touched on in earlier treatises. Some modern scholars believe they have detected in the treatises, arranged in chronological order, an intellectual development. It is true that we can notice different emphases at different times in Plotinus' life: for example, the confrontation with Gnosticism seems to have come to a head in the 260s and the last treatises show greater concentration on moral themes. Evolution in some areas of his philosophy might well have occurred. We should remember however that Plotinus started writing in his fifties, when his ideas can be expected to have reached some maturity. If his first compositions seem somewhat stiff and terse as compared to the freedom and depth of thought of the later works, this may have to do, not so much with intellectual development, as with growing confidence and ease with writing.

Short of reading everything, we can of course read a selection of treatises. In the following chapters I propose one such selection of treatises, some of them taken from Plotinus' earlier writing, some from his more complex work.

1

Soul and Body

1. The Doctrine of Two Worlds

To those who approach Plato's philosophy for the first time, the most striking aspect of it perhaps is its distinctive way of seeing reality. Plato's dialogues, in particular the *Phaedo*, *Phaedrus*, *Republic*, and *Timaeus*, encourage us to visualize reality as if it were divided into two worlds, the material world that we perceive around us with our senses (the 'sensible' world) and an immaterial world to which we have access only by thought or intellect (the 'intelligible' world). The material world is subject to never-ending change. Everything in it is in continuous process: bodies are unceasingly formed and dissolved and are incapable of maintaining a stable identity. Material things are too evanescent and ambiguous for anything true to be said or known about them. The immaterial world, by contrast, is all stability, permanence, eternity. It is populated, not by bodies in flux, but by 'Forms' (or 'Ideas'). These are immaterial beings possessing clear-cut and unchanging identities: the Form of beauty, for example, is beauty itself, beauty eternal, as compared with the fugitive suggestions of beauty in material things. The relation between the two worlds is such, it appears, that the material world is a shadowing forth, an imaging of the world of Forms. The material world exists only to the extent that it shares in the eternal being of the Forms, just as a shadow exists only as the shadow of something. To comprehend the world that we see, the theatre of shadows in which we live, we must discover in thought the eternal models which it reflects, the world of Forms.

In presenting the Platonic doctrine of two worlds, it is difficult to avoid suggesting what the sense of the doctrine might be. A literal reading of Plato's visual language might take it that Plato does in fact see above or beyond this physical universe another universe, a sort of philosopher's Eden of light, perfection, and immortality to which our souls long to escape. Another interpretation of the doctrine, warning us against taking Plato's visual descriptions too literally, might claim that the doctrine boils down to a distinction between conceptual categories (the Forms) and the data of sense-perception. But what did Plato himself really mean to say? What is the precise sense of the distinction he makes between Forms and physical objects, between immaterial and material reality? These questions remain open even today. Many different answers have been proposed. There seem to be many ways of making philosophical sense (or nonsense) of Plato's distinction.

The Middle Platonists do not on the whole show much originality in their approach to the subject. Alcinous presupposes a simple schoolroom distinction between two worlds, between sensible and intelligible reality, as a basic and unquestioned dogma of Platonism (see, for example, *Didaskalikos*, ch. 4; also Atticus, fragment 8, and Apuleius, *De Platone et eius dogmate*, ch. 6). Numenius discusses the subject more fully in his dialogue *On the Good* (fragments 3–8), but he merely embroiders on what can be found in some passages in Plato. Emphasizing the evanescence of corporeal things and the immutability of the immaterial, he insists that only the latter can be regarded as what exists in the fullest and truest sense, since it remains what it is and is not subject to dissipation as are bodies. Plotinus, however, breaks away from such platitudes in various ways. He tends to approach Plato's distinction in the context of a distinction between soul and body. The need to avoid confusing soul with body and the discovery of intellect as the origin of soul bring us to a new way of understanding the difference between immaterial and material reality. And the problem of the relation between these two kinds of reality arises in connection with the difficult problems posed by the link between soul and body. In this chapter Plotinus' interpretation of the doctrine of two worlds will be discussed in terms of the distinction between soul and body. The topic will be examined further in the following two chapters as regards the link between soul and body (Ch. 2) and the relation between soul and intellect (Ch. 3).

For almost 2,000 years many philosophers took for granted the Platonic belief that the visible world is the shadow of a higher, more substantial, immaterial world. Even Aristotelians, inasmuch as they believed in the existence of a superior, immaterial divine substance, came near to this view, although they did not follow the Platonists in condemning the material world to a sort of semi-existence. A decisive change and a new beginning came only in the seventeenth century, with René Descartes. In his effort to break away from ancient and medieval philosophy and found a new, resolutely modern philosophy Descartes took as the fundamental metaphysical distinction that between mind and body. The question whether 'mind' (however defined) is 'different' (and in what sense) from body (whatever that may be) remains unresolved and crucial in modern philosophy. To what extent did Plotinus, in interpreting the two-world doctrine as a distinction between soul (or intellect) and body, anticipate Descartes's new beginning? Some suggestions concerning this will be made in the conclusion to this chapter.

2. The Immortality of Soul (*Ennead* IV. 7 [2])

One of Plotinus' first writings, *Ennead* IV. 7 [2], is devoted to showing that the soul is immortal. Plato had argued for this in the *Phaedo* and in the *Phaedrus* (245ce). Plato's claim that soul is an incorporeal, non-composite reality not subject to destruction is rejected by Aristotle. For Aristotle, soul, as the structure (or 'form') responsible for the various functions of a living body, cannot escape death. Yet one living function, intellect, seems to be an exception: in Aristotle's view thinking is not the function of a particular bodily organ. Intellect thus seems to have a claim to immortality (*De anima*, 2. 2. 413^{b}24–7; 3. 4–5). However, Aristotle is at his most obscure here and in any case the question of immortality lies far from his primarily biological interests in the *De anima*. The Stoics on the whole admit only a limited and impersonal sort of immortality: after death the souls of the wise can become one with the divine spirit permeating the world. The Epicureans, true to their theory that all is nothing but a series of temporary groupings of atoms in the void, thought of soul as a grouping of (particularly fine) atoms, therefore of its very nature destined to disintegration. In IV. 7 Plotinus argues for Plato's position by disproving the theories of Aristotle, of the Stoics, and of the Epicureans. And this argument in turn has an effect, as we will see, on the kind of position that Plotinus ends up defending.

Plotinus quickly shows (ch. 1) how the question of immortality involves another question, that of the nature of soul. For if we are composed of body and soul, it is clearly only in soul that any real chance can be found of surviving death. But this would mean that soul cannot be body and must be able to exist without body. Plotinus therefore argues in chapters 2–8³ against the Stoic and Epicurean claim that soul is a body. If Aristotle does not identify soul with body, his approach nevertheless makes soul on the whole dependent on body for its existence, as does a version of Pythagoreanism which sees soul as a harmonious order of bodily parts. Plotinus must therefore argue against these positions also (chs. 8⁴–8⁵) before concluding (ch. 9) that soul is not a body and does not depend for its existence on body.

3. Soul is not Body (*Ennead* IV. 7. 2–8³)

Many of the arguments marshalled by Plotinus against the thesis of those, principally the Stoics, who identify soul as body are not new. They can be found already in Plato's *Phaedo*, in Aristotle's *De anima*, in the Aristotelian commentators, and in Middle Platonism. The overall strategy followed by Plotinus might be summarized in this way:

1. All parties involved in the debate agree that by 'soul' they mean the cause responsible for life in certain bodies (including plants and animals as well as humans).
2. The nature of body is not such as to make it capable of acting as such a cause.

By arguing for the second point, Plotinus has the basis for concluding that soul, as he and his opponents understand it, cannot be of bodily nature. The second point is shown both as regards life in general and as regards various specific living functions. A few examples of Plotinus' argument might be considered briefly here.

If soul is the source of life in a living body, it must itself have life. If it is body, then it is such as being one (or more) of the four basic constituents (or elements) of bodies—fire, air, water, and earth—or as being a compound produced from these elements. But the elements themselves are lifeless. And things compounded from the elements depend on something else, a cause that puts them together. But this something else is what is meant by soul. Therefore soul cannot be body, either as an element or as a combination of elements (ch. 2).

As for the various specific living functions, Plotinus follows the list of functions given by Aristotle in the *De anima*, a list that helps make concrete what is meant by 'life': to live is to be capable of one or more of the functions of nutrition, growth, reproduction, locomotion, sense-perception, imagination, memory, thought. In Plotinus' view it can be shown that soul, as the cause responsible for these particular functions, cannot be body. For example, 'How do we remember and how do we recognize those close to us if our souls never stay the same?' (5. 22–4). That is, how can I have an identity that persists through time if my soul is a body and all body is in perpetual flux? And when I perceive something, I perceive as one perceiver, and not as a multitude of different perceiving parts. The power to perceive acts both as a unity and as present throughout the different parts of the body. But a body cannot be in different places and not lose its unity. Therefore soul as the faculty of perception cannot be a body (chs. 6–7). And how could there be thinking of incorporeal entities if thought is the function of a body (ch. 8)?

Plotinus has many more arguments and of those mentioned above only the briefest of summaries has been given. The arguments would not have convinced the Stoics. They had after all attempted to explain how thinking takes place in a soul that is of bodily nature. Their conception of soul includes the idea of a unifying tensional force which binds together as a unity the different perceptual components in the body. And they did not subscribe to the theory of bodily nature which Plotinus assumes, a fairly common theory in Greek philosophy which can be found in Aristotle as well as in Plato, according to which bodies are made up from four basic inanimate elements. The Stoics spoke rather of a corporeal force, a sort of cosmic life-giving spirit or breath (*pneuma*) which penetrates and organizes a purely passive matter, creating increasingly complex levels of material reality culminating in rationality. Plotinus, however, takes for granted his own conception of body. He thus assumes that body is incapable of self-movement, of self-organization. It does not have the power to create higher, in particular organic, functions. These functions must be produced by something different, which therefore cannot be a body.

Yet the argument with the Stoics was not fruitless. It encouraged Plotinus to think of soul as a cosmic force that unifies, organizes, sustains, and controls every aspect of the world. It is true that Plato had spoken in the *Timaeus* of a cosmic soul (34b–37c). The importance which this idea takes on in Plotinus suggests that new light had been thrown on it in the confrontation with Stoicism.

4. Soul does not Depend on Body (*Ennead* IV. 7. 8⁴–8⁵)

Having disposed to his satisfaction of the claim that soul is body, Plotinus next turns to the thesis that soul, if incorporeal, nevertheless depends on its relation to body in order to exist. Speaking of the notion that soul is a certain harmonious order of bodily parts Plotinus asks what is responsible for so arranging the parts: soul? But then soul is not the order, but rather that which makes the order (ch. 8⁴). And if soul is the form or structure of a certain kind of body, as Aristotle claims, then what of thinking, a living function which Aristotle himself does not regard as the function of a particular bodily part. Plotinus suggests that even the lower biological functions are not tied to particular bodily organs as functions of them. The example he gives is that of a plant which can retain its various biological powers in its root even when the parts of its body corresponding to these powers are withered (ch. 8⁵).

Plotinus' criticism of Aristotle is scarcely more convincing than his attack on Stoicism, although it is true, as he suggests, that there are very real difficulties in reconciling Aristotle's analysis of thinking with the rest of his psychology (on this see already Atticus, fragment 7). Plotinus' argument here is in any case very brief. After the long struggle with Stoic materialism he hastens to the desired end, the conclusion that soul, as the source of life in bodies, is not a body and does not depend on body for its existence. This in turn points to the immortality of soul. Plotinus is quick also to convert the distinction he has established between soul and body into a broad distinction between intelligible and sensible reality, or, in the words of Plato's *Timaeus* (28a), between what is truly and eternally and what is subject to perpetual change (ch. 8^5. 46–50; ch. 9).

This broadening of the distinction between soul and body requires far more careful attention than it is given at the end of IV. 7. Plotinus himself indicates that many questions remain to be answered. Does the argument for immortality concern soul taken in general or also each individual soul (ch. 12)? If soul is separate from body, how does it come about that it enters body (ch. 13)? Are the souls of plants and animals immortal (ch. 14)? What of the three parts of the soul of which Plato speaks in the *Republic*—do they all survive death (ch. 14)? Plotinus discusses these questions very briefly and answers some of them; he will come back to a fuller discussion of some of them in later treatises, as we will see.

5. The Concept of Soul in *Ennead* IV. 7

The arguments in IV. 7 for the distinction between soul and body and for the independence of soul *vis-à-vis* the body might strike us sometimes as sketchy and polemical. The treatise does however help to show how Plotinus' version of Platonism was affected by the challenge represented by competing philosophies, in particular those of Aristotle and of the Stoics. No doubt Plotinus regards himself as merely defending Plato by means of disarming the adversaries. But his Plato is reshaped by the debate. Soul in Plotinus behaves much like the Stoic cosmic life-force which permeates passive matter, giving it structure, cohesion, order in every respect and detail. Furthermore the specific functions exercised by this dynamic cause correspond to those listed by Aristotle. At the same time Plotinus distances himself from Stoicism and Aristotelianism. Body in general, as the inanimate basic elements or as compounded from them, is characterized by the passivity, the incapacity for self-organization that the Stoics attributed to only one aspect of corporeal nature. This is why the dynamic force without which the world could not exist must, for Plotinus, be incorporeal and independent of body. As for Aristotelianism, Plotinus does not restrict the realm of soul to organic things, as does Aristotle: soul, for Plotinus, is responsible for the structure of the entire universe. Nor does he understand the different functions exercised by soul as necessarily existing only as the functions of the corresponding bodily organs. Soul can act in different ways in relation to different organs of the body. But it does not depend on these organs in order to exist. This may suffice at present as a preliminary sketch of Plotinus' concept of soul. The following chapters will examine other issues that will allow us to develop our sketch in various ways.

6. Plotinus and Descartes

To what extent did Plotinus, in approaching the doctrine of two worlds in the light of the distinction between soul and body, anticipate the new foundation that Descartes wished to give to modern science and philosophy, that is, the distinction between mind and body? A link between the two philosophers cannot be excluded. One of Plotinus' most intelligent and enthusiastic readers in antiquity was (for a while at least) St Augustine. Augustine's works illustrate vividly the Plotinian approach to immaterial reality as the discovery of the nature of soul and of its origin. Augustine was also the greatest of the Latin Church Fathers and his works formed part of the intellectual atmosphere of the educated Christian in Descartes's age. Indeed some of Descartes's contemporaries were struck by the closeness of some of his ideas to those of Augustine.

There are, however, important differences between Plotinus' version of the doctrine of two worlds and Descartes's distinction between mind and body. Descartes wished to construct a chain of scientific truths possessing absolute certitude. This meant discounting at first all impressions derived from sense-perception. The very first certitude, he found, was that of his own existence as mind, a certitude which did not necessarily entail certitude as to his existence as body. If Descartes later shows the existence of body, it is clear that the relation between mind and body is not such that mind is wholly responsible for all bodily functions: most living functions are the work of the body and arise from bodily mechanisms. Plotinus, on the other hand, is not primarily concerned with elaborating an invincible series of certitudes, but is more interested in the world and how it comes to be organized as it is, of course with the purpose of reaching the truth about this. And the soul which he finds, forming and sustaining the world as it does in every detail, is very different from Descartes's mind.

There are, however, other ways in which Plotinus anticipated to some extent, I believe, the new direction Descartes gave to philosophy. Descartes's attempt to elaborate scientific knowledge on the basis, not of the observation of the world, but of what can be determined with certitude from the analysis of the mind, led to an interest in what might be called the problem of human subjectivity, a problem characteristic of modern philosophy. Far from simply observing and describing the world, as might be done in a 'naïve' approach, the modern philosopher raises questions about the human subject who is pursuing such observations. What does this subject presuppose in his research? What does he inject in the methods used to analyse the world? To know the world we must find out more about the nature of the human mind that seeks to know. Plotinus is keenly aware that his enquiries involve not only the object being discussed, the world, but also the human subject who enquires and discusses. He indicates toward the end of IV. 7 (ch. 10) that the questions treated are by no means of remote concern. To discover that soul is independent of body, that body derives what structure and value it has from soul, is to discover something of essential importance to oneself. When we examine the world, we are expressing and discovering our true self as soul. And the discovery of our true self leads both to further exploration of what is implicit in this self and to a better understanding of the world that we, as soul, produce.

Plotinus anticipates Descartes and modern philosophy in yet another way. Although he speaks of intelligible reality as 'above' or 'beyond' the material world, he is quite clear that this relation is not to be understood in spatial terms. Intelligible reality is discovered within ourselves, as soul, and further investigation of the roots of our nature discloses the primary form of intelligible being, intellect. In a sense Plotinus internalizes intelligible reality, as opposed to an externalizing conception that sees it as another world outside and beyond this world. For Plotinus intelligible reality is to be found in the depths of our own nature. This internalization of the intelligible is characteristic of modern philosophy, where it lacks, however, the cosmic significance it has in Plotinus: if intelligible principles are to be found within us, these principles do not, it is assumed, produce the world.

2

The Relation between Sensible
and Intelligible Reality

1. How is Soul Present in Body (*Ennead* VI. 4–5 [22–3])?

The distinction Plotinus makes between soul and body in IV. 7 leaves some matters unresolved and leads to other questions. The identification of this distinction with that between intelligible and sensible reality requires further discussion: in Chapter 3 below it will be seen that intelligible reality includes not just soul but also other entities. Furthermore, given Plotinus' distinction between soul and body, one might wonder *why* soul, if it is so different from body, finds itself in body, and indeed *how* soul could ever be present in body. This last question provoked much debate in Plotinus' school, for Porphyry tells us: 'For three days I, Porphyry, asked him [Plotinus] how soul is with the body and he persisted in his explanation' (*Life of Plotinus*, 13. 11–12). What was it that made this so hard to understand? Why should the way in which soul is present in body be so puzzling?

Ennead VI. 4–5 [22–3], the first work Plotinus composed after Porphyry's arrival in the school, shows how Plotinus would have tried to answer Porphyry. The first chapter presents the problem, which might be formulated as follows. The distinction between soul and body means that the one possesses a nature very different from that of the other. Body is composite, made up ultimately of the four elements (fire, air, water, and earth), which themselves are constituted of form and matter. As composite, body tends by nature towards disintegration. It is characterized furthermore by the possession of size, mass, and is tied to place such that it cannot be in different places without being dispersed, different parts occupying different places. Soul, on the other hand, is non-composite, not subject to disintegration, and, as incorporeal, has no size or mass. Nor is it localized, or tied to place, as body is. But if we say, with Plotinus, that soul is *present* in body, how could such presence be possible? If soul is present everywhere in the body in such a way that it is spread out over the different parts and places in body, must not this divide up soul? And if soul is to remain one, how could it preserve this unity and yet be present at the same time as a whole in different places in the body? Is Plotinus' distinction between soul and body so strong that it becomes difficult to see how they could ever be related to each other, notwithstanding his insistence that soul makes body into everything that it is?

In VI. 4. 2 Plotinus connects the problem of soul's presence in body with a larger issue, that of the presence of intelligible reality in the sensible world. He is aware that in doing this he is confronting one of the most difficult problems facing any Platonist. Among the difficulties presented by Plato in his *Parmenides* concerning the theory of Forms is that of the presence of a single Form in a multitude of particular sensible objects (131ac): how could one Form (for example, the Form of beauty) be present in many (beautiful) things without being divided up among them? The presence of the Form in a multitude seems to mean destruction of the Form as a whole, as a unity. This cannot be right. But to save the Form's unity, one must abandon its presence in many things. This too is unacceptable. Plato himself gives no clear indication as to how one is to resolve this dilemma. Aristotle considered it as yet another decisive reason for rejecting Plato's theory of Forms (*Metaphysics*, 1. 6). The problem remained unresolved, lying deep, as a possibly fatal flaw, in the heart of Platonic philosophy. The Middle Platonists were aware of it, but they contented themselves with references to the 'mysterious' relation between intelligible and sensible reality. Plotinus' *Ennead* VI. 4–5 is the first Platonist text we have which faces the issue squarely.

2. A Category Mistake

In reading VI. 4–5, one might pick out various aspects of Plotinus' approach to the problem of presence. One aspect consists in the analysis of the problem as arising from what could be described as a 'category mistake': we are puzzled about how an immaterial nature can be present as a whole in many separate bodies or bodily parts because we make the mistake of thinking of this immaterial nature *as if* it must behave just as do bodies, that is, that it cannot be spread over different places without being divided up. And indeed the notion, a Stoic one, that a body can be dispersed throughout other bodies and yet retain its unity is for Plotinus an impossible one. The problem of presence can then be diagnosed as arising from a mental confusion which consists (1) in thinking of immaterial being as subject to the same restrictions, in particular local restrictions, as bodies, and consequently (2) not seeing how an immaterial being can be present as a whole throughout body.

But an account attempting to examine what is being said and which is not a unity, but something divided, bringing into the enquiry the nature of bodies whence it derives its principles, this account fragmented being, thinking it is like this, and doubted its unity since it [the account] did not initiate the enquiry from the appropriate principles. (VI. 5. 2. 1–6)

The diagnosis points to an appropriate therapy: accustoming oneself to thinking of immaterial being in another way, not as if it were body, but in the light of its proper, non-quantitative, non-local characteristics. Much of VI. 4–5 is devoted to this therapy. Again and again Plotinus comes back to the same ideas, examining them from different angles, helping the reader develop habits of thought that will make him less inclined to confusion. We might say then that the problem of the presence of soul in body, of the intelligible in the sensible, derives from a flaw, not in Plato's philosophy, but in our understanding of it. Learning to think correctly will eliminate the problem.

But not entirely. There is reason to believe that, even if one reads VI. 4–5 many times over and exercises oneself so as to avoid category mistakes, the problem will not be completely removed. For if a given intelligible nature is not present in various bodies in the way that a body is present in other bodies, then in what sense is it present? Does not 'presence' mean being localized in a particular body? What could 'immaterial presence' possibly be?

3. The Self-Presence of the Intelligible

Plotinus develops some ideas in VI. 4–5 which might help here. In particular he attempts to formulate what 'presence' might mean when spoken of in regard to immaterial being. As he suggests in VI. 5. 2, we must try to think of immaterial being, not in terms of the categories that apply to bodies, but in terms of those relevant to its particular nature:

But we, for the account of what is one and total being, must adopt principles appropriate to conviction, that is intelligible principles pertaining to the intelligibles and to true being. For since the one kind [i.e. bodies] is subject to motion and all sorts of changes and is divided up over all places, what would appropriately be called 'becoming' and not 'being', whereas the other kind [i.e. intelligible being] is eternally unchanging being, neither generated nor destroyed, having no location or place or base, not coming from somewhere or going somewhere, but staying in itself, when one speaks of the former [kind], one should reason from this nature and from what is judged concerning it, probabilities based on probabilities, making arguments that are also probable in character. But when one discusses the intelligibles, one would do well to take as principles of one's account the nature of being with which one is concerned, not deviating, as if having forgotten, to another nature. (VI. 5. 2. 6–22)

Following these injunctions we can develop a description of immaterial being that singles out its unchangingness, its independence from any particular place or body 'in' which it would exist, a perfection of existence that excludes its 'going away' from itself to be in another, a self-dispersal such as marks corporeal nature:

If then real [intelligible] being is this, unchanging, not departing from itself, subject to no process of becoming, not being said to be in place, it must always be as it is and with itself, not departing from itself, nor a part of it being here and another part there, nothing issuing from it—for then it would already be in another and in another, and in general in something, and not by itself and free from being affected, for it would be affected if it were in another, but to be unaffected it must not be in another. (VI. 5. 3. 1–8)

We might say then that there is the presence of bodies, which is their dispersal throughout different places, and the presence of immaterial being, which is its self-integrity: as the presence to others of a body can be seen in the light of its dependent unstable nature tending perpetually to dispersion, so the totally unified and stable nature of the intelligible constitutes a kind of complete presence to itself. This is the complete presence of a multiplicity to itself, for there are many intelligibles, as we will see below in Chapter 3. But the many intelligibles are not separated from each other by differences in place (VI. 4. 4). The perfection of their existence constitutes a kind of total presence of each to each other.

In this way Plotinus gives some content to the concept of immaterial presence, a concept which otherwise would seem to have little sense. We may still however be dissatisfied. For Plotinus has distinguished the presence of bodies to each other from the presence to itself of immaterial being. But our problem concerns the presence of an immaterial being such as soul to bodies.

4. Presence as Dependence

In VI. 4–5 Plotinus explores other ideas that bring us nearer to a solution. The most important, I think, is the interpretation he proposes of the word 'in', in so far as it concerns the relation between immaterial and material reality. In Greek 'in' can mean to be 'in' someone's or something's power, to be dependent on this power. In this sense immaterial being is 'in' nothing as not depending on any body for its existence. On the other hand body, as dependent on soul, can be said to be 'in' soul, just as material reality depends on, or is 'in', immaterial being (VI. 4. 2). This explains, for Plotinus, why Plato, in the *Timaeus* (36de), places the body of the world 'in' soul.

In VI. 4. 7 Plotinus gives an illustration, the example of a hand holding some object: the hand is present as a whole throughout the object as the power on which the object depends, in which it lies. Another illustration is given in a slightly later work, *Ennead* IV. 3 [27]:

For the universe lies in soul which sustains it, and nothing is without having some share in soul, as if a net were to live plunged in water but not able to possess that in which it is. But wherever the net is, as much as it can, it spreads with the sea which is already extended, for each of its parts cannot be in any other place than where it lies, whereas soul is in its nature so great that it is not of a certain size, so that it can hold all body with the same part and wherever body is spread, soul is there. (IV. 3. 9. 36–44)

In other words, Plotinus asks us to reverse our normal way of thinking. We should not think of soul as being somehow 'in' body. In this sense the question as to how soul is in body is badly put. Such is the relation between soul and body that we should try rather to conceive of body as being 'in' soul, in the sense that it depends entirely for its organization and life on soul. A similar reversal is brought about when Plotinus, in VI. 4–5, speaks, not of soul 'going' to, or 'descending into', body, but of body as going to, or approaching, soul. This overturning of the old ways of speaking of the relation of soul and body is intended to free us of spatial conceptions of the relation: body 'going to' soul means its depending on soul for its existence as body.

Many particular bodies can be 'in' the one immaterial nature in the sense that they can all depend on that one nature. This dependence can be varied in relation to the variety of bodies and of their particular capacities (VI. 4. 12). But the immaterial force on which they depend remains 'in' itself as a whole, an integral totality, not divided up by the dependence of various bodies on it.

5. A Dilemma Resolved?

It might be useful to reflect on Plotinus' solution, such as it emerges in VI. 4–5, to the problem of the presence of the immaterial in the material. In facing this problem directly, was he successful in disarming one of the major objections to Plato's view of reality? Have the dilemmas of the *Parmenides* and Aristotle's criticisms really been overcome?

The problem, Plotinus suggests, concerns not only Platonic philosophers and their critics: 'That the one and the same in number is everywhere and at the same time whole is a common notion, one might say, when all men are moved of themselves to say that the god in each of us is one and the same' (VI. 5. 1. 1–4). If men assume the presence of one god among them, then they must assume a presence of the type Plotinus wishes to elucidate. Can they defend and explain their assumption? St Augustine was quick to take up this suggestion and applies Plotinus' ideas on immaterial presence to the explanation of the presence of the Christian god in the world and among men:

> We have, therefore, in the truth [i.e. God] a possession which we can all enjoy equally and in common; there is nothing wanting or defective in it . . . It is a food which is never divided; you drink nothing from it which I cannot drink. When you share in it, you make nothing your private possession; what you take from it still remains whole for me too . . . it is wholly common to all at the same time. Therefore what we touch, or taste, or smell, are less like the truth than what we hear and see. Every word is heard wholly by all who hear it, and wholly by each at the same time, and every sight presented to the eyes is seen as much by one man as by another at the same time. But the likeness [i.e. between the presence of audible or visual objects and the presence of God] is a very distant one.[1]

Augustine's examples, the one sound heard and the one sight seen by all, come from Plotinus (VI. 4, 12; III. 8. 9).

Whatever its broader implications, Plotinus' solution to the problem of presence is persuasive, I think, to the extent that the reader already subscribes to the claim that there exists another type of reality, immaterial being, from which this world around us derives its characteristics. If one holds to this view, then the problem of presence can be treated along the lines Plotinus suggests. That is, the problem of presence need no longer represent for the Platonist a

[1] *De libero arbitrio*, 2. 14. 37–8, trans. M. Pontifex, *St. Augustine: The Problem of Free Choice* (Westminster, Md., 1955).

mystery, a philosophical embarrassment, a skeleton in his meta-physical cupboard. On the other hand, if one denies the existence of immaterial being, one can hardly be satisfied with Plotinus' discussion, since it takes its principles from the assumption of such an existence.

The critic of Platonism might wonder furthermore how much really has been gained by reading the relation of presence (of the immaterial in the material) as a relation of dependence (of the material on the immaterial). How helpful is it to say that soul is present in body in the sense that body depends on soul? The relation of dependence is one of cause and effect. Such a causal relation seems to sidestep the local relationship expressed by the concept of presence. But does it really? Are not causal relations relations between bodies that are in spatial contact with each other? So might argue an ancient critic of Platonic immaterialism, a Stoic for example (we might prefer today to speak of causal relations, not as bodies in contact with and acting on bodies, but as events coming under certain laws). What might Plotinus' response have been?

6. How does Soul Act on Body?

The Stoics affirmed that only body could act as a cause on body (it was a reason for them for identifying soul as body). This principle had already been formulated by Aristotle. According to him, one object, to act on another, must in general be in physical contact with it, that is, both must be in local proximity to each other and both of course must be bodies. In this sense soul, as an incorporeal entity, cannot act on body. It is not surprising then that Aristotle (*De anima*, 1. 3) finds that Plato, in making soul into a reality separate from body, is unable to explain how soul acts on body, although such an action is clearly assumed. This inability to explain soul's action on body undermines the Platonist's concept of soul since it obliges him, it seems, to abandon either his separation of soul from body or his belief that soul acts on body. His position as a whole becomes untenable.

Much the same criticism has been made of Descartes's distinction between mind and body. He too has been found to be unable to explain how mind acts on body although he clearly presupposes such action. In a notorious passage Descartes shows he is aware of the problem, although it hardly seems to worry him:

And I may say . . . that the question that your Majesty proposes seems to me the one that one can put with most justification, in view of the writings I have published. For there are two points [concerning soul] . . . one is that it thinks, the other that being united to the body the soul can act and suffer with it. I have said little or nothing about the second point and have tried only to make clear the first. (Letter to Princess Elizabeth, 21 May 1643)

Whatever Descartes's solution might have been, it is clear that Plotinus could hardly ignore the problem since it had been raised in Aristotle's criticism of Plato.

Plotinus does not discuss the question of how soul acts on body at any great length in any treatise. But we can find passages that contain the elements of an answer. He would not agree then that no answer can be given to the critic of Platonism. And what he suggests by way of an answer goes a good deal further than the few unhelpful indications to be found on the subject in Plato, in particular in the *Laws* (10. 897a, 898e–899a).

A first point that Plotinus makes is that soul's action whereby body is changed must be distinguished from the change produced in body by this action. For example soul as the cause of growth in a body does not, in causing this change in body, itself grow:

For the part of soul responsible for growth, in causing growth, does not grow, nor in bringing increase does it increase, nor in general in causing movement does it move with the movement [or change, *kinesis*] it causes, but it does not move at all, or if it does, with another type of movement or activity [*energeia*]. So this nature of the form must be activity and must make by its presence. (III. 6 [26]. 4. 38–42)

To express the difference between soul's action and the bodily changes it produces Plotinus adopts in this passage the distinction that Aristotle makes between activity and movement or change. For Aristotle, something changes when it has not yet realized its potential for functioning in a certain way, but is in the process of reaching this realization which, once achieved, is its activity. For example, we change when we learn to become musicians; we are in activity as musicians when we possess and use this art. Change is thus linked to incompletion, imperfection, partial approximation to full functioning which is activity. For Plotinus, however, the distinction between change and activity expresses the difference between an imperfect approximation in bodily conditions to a perfect functioning characteristic of soul as an incorporeal nature. In Aristotle activity is the normal culmination of change; in Plotinus it is the independent functioning of immaterial reality from which bodily changes result as imperfect imitations.

Plotinus gives as an example the relation between a tune and the tune as it is played on strings: 'For there [when strings are played] it is not the tune that is affected, but the string. But the string would not have been moved, even if the musician wished it, unless the tune directed it' (III. 6. 4. 49–52). Plotinus' chief concern here is to keep separate the immaterial, non-spatial, non-temporal, non-quantitative activities proper to the nature of soul from the various bodily changes produced by these activities. But how are these changes produced? The musical example is not a good one. For the tune is produced in the strings by a third factor, the player acting as agent, but soul is not only the tune but also the agent of bodily changes. How then does it produce them?

Aristotle's analysis of change in the world provides Plotinus with concepts that are useful here. According to Aristotle, if something changes, that is, moves towards the realization of an activity for which it has the potential, it can only do this if the goal of the process, the activity, is already present in some way at the start of the change in order to give it direction. Thus we learn to become musicians from a teacher who already possesses the art and directs us to it. In this way the activity that is the goal of a change must precede the change. In the physical universe this means that every change presupposes a prior activity that is independent of it, the whole system of changes and activities depending ultimately on a pure (i.e. changeless) activity, divine immaterial substance, that guarantees the eternity of the system. Aristotle, it seems, thinks of the heavenly bodies as contemplating this divine substance, and, inspired by its perfection (pure activity), imitating it in their eternal circular motions. These motions bring about in turn the unceasing processes on earth.

Plotinus adopted this model of causal relations to the extent that soul, for him, is also an immaterial activity that produces corporeal changes, not as one body pushing or pulling another, but as a prior independent perfection that inspires imitations which are corporeal changes. Or, rather, the different living functions in a body are changes, taking place in appropriate organs, relating to corresponding prior activities characteristic of soul.

Another problem, that concerning the making of the world (below, Chapter 7), will provide an opportunity for returning to the complex question of soul's action on body. Perhaps comments similar to those proposed above in section 5 could be made concerning Plotinus' discussion of the question of soul's action on body. In Plotinus' favour one might note that he keeps rigorously to his distinction between soul and body. He does not compromise this distinction by having soul behave as if it were a body, that is, as if it could act on body by physical or mechanical means. If only the resort to such means can satisfy a critic, for example a Stoic, who puts the question of soul's action on body, then the critic is asking that Plotinus abandon the distinction between soul and body. Plotinus furthermore makes astute use of concepts that occur in the physics of Plato's greatest pupil and most formidable critic, Aristotle, since these concepts allow for causal relations between the immaterial and the material. As the many changes in Aristotle's universe depend on an independent immaterial substance, so in Plotinus do they depend on soul.

3

Soul, Intellect, and the Forms

1. Soul and Intellect (*Ennead* V. 9 [5]. 1–4)

In Chapter 1 above the distinction between intelligible and sensible
reality has been approached from the point of view of the distinction
between soul and body. The discussion of problems that any
Platonist must face, of criticisms made by Aristotelians and Stoics,
led Plotinus to a new way of looking at the distinction and relation
between soul and body. While quickly concluding that his results
concerned the relation between intelligible and sensible reality in
general, he believed that soul constituted only a part of intelligible
being. In this chapter the differences *within* intelligible reality will be
explored in connection with the analysis of two problems: the
relation between soul and intellect (*nous*); and the relation between
intellect and the Forms. I shall refer in what follows to 'divine
intellect' so as to indicate that Plotinus is thinking primarily, not of
human intellect, but of an intellect which is independent of the
world and is presupposed by the soul which produces the world.

The notion that we must postulate a divine intellect in order to
explain the world as a rational structure is common enough in Greek
philosophy. The Stoics think of their immanent organizing god as
rational, as *logos*, of which we, as minds, are fragments. This *logos*
guarantees that the world it structures is open to understanding,
rational. A divine intellect of cosmic significance also appears in
Aristotelian philosophy. The divine immaterial substance imitated
by the heavens is described by Aristotle as an intellect which thinks
(*Metaphysics*, 12. 7, 9), presumably because Aristotle knows of no
other activity that is independent of body. This divine intellect

assumes even greater importance in Aristotle's commentator Alexander of Aphrodisias. In trying to explain a desperately obscure chapter in Aristotle's *De anima* (3. 5), which speaks of our potential to think as being brought to activity by an agent, an active intellect, Alexander identifies this agent with the divine intellect of *Metaphysics*, 12. Thus god both brings us to thought and inspires imitation of his perfection in the universe. Finally the Middle Platonists often speak of a divine intellect. However, their views are by no means clearly worked out. They found a divine intellect in Plato's *Timaeus*, the divine artisan (or 'demiurge') who fashions the world after the model provided by the Forms (28a–29b). But what is the relation between this divine intellect and the Forms? And what might the relation be between this intellect and the supreme cause mentioned in Plato's *Republic* (509b), the 'Form of the Good'? Alcinous suggests one approach: the Forms are nothing else than the thoughts of a divine intellect that transcends the world, an intellect which looks very much like Aristotle's god. An inferior intellect, that of a world-soul, contemplates the higher intellect and is inspired by this model in ordering the world (*Didaskalikos*, chs. 10, 12, 14). There are difficulties in this interpretation of Plato, as we will see, and it was not the only one put forward by Platonists.

At any rate we can say that although most philosophers in antiquity postulated the existence of a divine intellect of cosmic importance, there was much disagreement among them as to how this intellect should be described. 'Now perhaps it is ridiculous to ask if there is intellect, although some might even argue about that. Rather it is our task to speak about whether intellect is of the kind we say it is, if there is a separate intellect and if this is the true beings and if the nature of true Forms is there' (V. 9 [5]. 3. 4–8). Plotinus sets out therefore in the earlier chapters of *Ennead* V. 9 [5] to argue for the existence of a divine intellect of a certain kind, one that (1) is separate from the universe (against the Stoics) and (2) constitutes a unity with the Forms, or 'true beings' (against the Aristotelians and some Platonists). Several lines of thought lead to this conclusion; we might briefly consider one of them (V. 9. 3–4).

Returning to the claim that soul organizes the world (see above, Chapter 1), we can add that this activity presupposes an 'art', that is a body of knowledge, a wisdom, which guides it. The wisdom shown by soul, Plotinus argues, in its ordering of things is not one belonging by nature to soul. Soul is 'informed' with this wisdom: soul can acquire and can lose it. Or, to speak in terms which bring us close to Alexander of Aphrodisias' reading of Aristotle's *De anima*, soul is brought to the activity that is wisdom by a prior agent, an intellect which must be independent of it and of the world as that which inspires soul in making the world. This independent intellect does not receive wisdom, or become wise, for else we would have to postulate yet another independent intellect which would inform it and which would itself be wisdom at its source.

The argument thus leads to the conclusion (1) that the divine intellect presupposed by the rational organization of the world by soul must be independent of the world, contrary to the opinion of the Stoics, so as to be the source of the wisdom which informs soul's action; and (2) that this intellect has as its inherent activity wisdom, that is, knowledge of the Forms which are the models followed by soul. This last claim stands in opposition both to Aristotelians, who denied the existence of the Forms, and to certain Platonists, who interpreted the relation between divine intellect and the Forms in other ways. The latter point requires further attention.

2. Intellect and the Forms (*Ennead* V. 9. 5–8)

We know that there was considerable disagreement among Platonists in Plotinus' time about the relation between the divine intellect and the Forms. The occasion that provoked the debate was provided by a difficult text in Plato's *Timaeus* (39e), to which Plotinus refers in the following passage:

'Intellect', [Plato] says, 'sees the Forms that are in the [ideal] animal'. Then the maker [the demiurge], he says, 'reasoned that that which the intellect sees in the [ideal] animal, this universe should also have'. Is he saying that the Forms existed prior to intellect, and that intellect thinks them as they already exist? (III. 9 [13]. 1, 1–5)

At issue here is the independence of the Forms. The interpretation Plotinus mentions makes the Forms prior to the divine intellect, that is, they exist independently of the intellect that thinks them. They are before, or 'outside', the intellect. This option was defended in Plotinus' school by Porphyry until he was persuaded to abandon it (*Life of Plotinus*, 18. 10–19). Porphyry's former teacher in Athens, Longinus, held to another view, that the Forms are posterior to the divine intellect. A third opinion, that defended by Plotinus, is found already in Alcinous, who identifies the divine intellect with the Forms in such a way that the Forms are the thoughts, the thinking activity, of the divine intellect (*Didaskalikos*, chs. 9–10). Plotinus supports this position in V. 9. 5. His argument runs roughly along the following lines.

Given the existence of an intellect independent of the world (a position common to all Aristotelians and Platonists), this intellect must have itself as the object of its thinking. The point had already been made by Aristotle (*Metaphysics*, 12. 9): if the divine intellect were to think something other than ('outside') itself, this would mean that the intellect at some point would only potentially know what is other than it . But no potentiality may be allowed to creep into what of necessity must be pure activity. Plotinus separates himself however from Aristotle when he claims that this self-thought in divine intellect is a thinking of the Forms. He claims this essentially because intellect functions for him as the origin of the wisdom, or prototypes, guiding soul in making the world. Such wisdom cannot be derived from the world, since it is the world's model, nor is it to be found originally in soul, which acquires it, nor can it be acquired by intellect as something other than (or outside) it, for this would admit potentiality into the divine intellect.

Several objections could be raised here. For example, in interpreting the Forms as the thoughts of a divine intellect, is there not a danger of making the Forms depend for their existence on their being thought by intellect? Does this not mean that intellect in effect 'thinks up' the Forms? Does this not contradict Plato's insistence on the independent reality of the Forms? Plotinus discusses this objection in V. 9. 7–8. He does not regard it as serious. The independence of the Forms can be preserved if divine thought is understood as the activity of the Forms. The Forms are not 'dead' objects: they have a life which is their activity and this activity is thought. As the Forms are 'true being', that is, possess an existence free of the evanescence characteristic of sensible things, this being is that of the thinking activity that is the Forms. And as there are many Forms whose activity is thought, we may speak of many intellects composing the unity of divine intellect and its object of thought.

This suggests yet another problem. Is it not self-contradictory to say both that divine intellect is one, as thinking itself, and that it is many, as the multiplicity of Forms which is its object of thought? How can the divine intellect be both one and many? In V. 9. 6 Plotinus suggests ways of lifting this contradiction without abandoning his position. The multiplicity proper to divine intellect is not spatially articulated: the several intelligible objects (or intellects) are not separated from each other by space in the way bodies are. They are 'all together', constituting the total co-presence and multiple unity explored in VI. 4–5 (above, Ch. 2 s. 3). Such a multiple unity is not altogether implausible, since other multiple unities are known to us on more familiar levels of experience: the seed is one and yet includes the variety of powers which manifest themselves as the seed develops; scientific knowledge is a systematic whole, a unity which is also a number of discrete theorems.

Ennead V. 9 concludes with the mention of other related questions which Plotinus discusses briefly (V. 9. 9–14): How many Forms are there? Of what sensible things are there Forms? Of the ugly? Of the non-natural? Of individuals? Before commenting in general on Plotinus' thesis of the pre-existence of a divine intellect in relation to soul and his thesis of the identity of this intellect with the Forms, we might consider other contexts in which the latter idea in particular is explored further.

3. The Problem of Truth (*Ennead* V. 5 [32]. 1–2)

Ennead V. 9 [5], one of Plotinus' first works, seems fairly simple and somewhat scholastic if compared to the two treatises, *Enneads* V. 5 [32] and V. 3 [49], which will be considered in part in what follows.

Only a brief indication can be given here of the philosophical subtlety and depth that await the reader of these two treatises.

At the beginning of *Ennéad* V. 5 Plotinus discusses the problem of truth, that is, the question whether or not we can claim to attain true knowledge. This text is part of a much larger work that Plotinus wrote in response to the challenge represented by Gnosticism (see above, Introduction, s. 1). Gnosticism exerted increasing influence on the minds of some of the members of Plotinus' school. To combat this influence Plotinus had his closest pupils prepare anti-Gnostic tracts (Porphyry, *Life of Plotinus*, ch. 16) and criticized Gnosticism himself, in particular in the large work composed of *Enneads* III. 8, V. 8, V. 5, and II. 9 (see above, Introduction, s. 2). In the last part of this work Plotinus formulates his views on Gnosticism: he sees it as a perverse reading of Plato which makes unjustified innovations, thus falsifying ancient wisdom. The Gnostic attitude is one of proud self-assertion, of refusal to understand, of self-imposed ignorance. Plotinus therefore seeks, not so much to argue with the Gnostics (a waste of time, he feels), as to counteract their influence by deepening his pupils' philosophical understanding.

In V. 5. 1–2 a fuller understanding is sought of the nature of truth. Rather than discussing the subject as it occurs in Gnosticism—an important Gnostic claim was that the maker (or demiurge) of the world acted in ignorance and error, thus producing a world not based on true knowledge—Plotinus recalls the arguments of Sceptic philosophy against the possibility of truth (V. 5. 1). The Sceptics had attacked philosophers, in particular the Stoics and Epicureans, who thought that sense-perception yielded true knowledge. How, the Sceptics asked, if sense-perception is a process whereby we acquire images representing objects, can we be sure of the truth of these images? The images could reflect aspects of our perceptual organs (if our eyes are bleary, for example) rather than faithfully representing objects. And we cannot verify the truth of perceptual images, since this verification would depend itself on perceptual images. If thinking is supposed to help us discern between true and false perceptual images, as it does in Stoicism, then difficulties arise here too. Thinking can be analysed as a process of reasoning (deduction) starting from premisses which are known in another way. But how? On the basis of perceptual images? Non-deductive premisses seem to be a kind of image or impression. But we cannot get around these images or impressions to verify their truth. The Sceptics conclude that man can make no claim to posses true knowledge.

Plotinus seems in V. 5. 1 to accept the arguments of the Sceptics as valid. But he does not feel obliged to reach the same conclusion, since the arguments rest on an assumption which he rejects. It is assumed by the Sceptic (and his opponents) that, in all cases of claims to true knowledge, the object known is exterior to (or other than) the subject who knows. To defend the possibility of truth, in Plotinus' view, we must reject this assumption. The possibility of true knowledge can be realized if the object known is the same as the subject that knows: 'So that the real truth agrees, not with another, but with itself, and does not say something else besides itself, but what it says, it is, and what it is, it says' (V. 5. 2. 18–20). In other words, the possibility of truth depends on the thesis that there exists a divine intellect whose object of thought is itself. This thesis, however difficult it may be to comprehend, is a necessary postulate if the claim to know anything is to be defended against the criticisms of the Sceptic philosopher.

We may feel that Plotinus is too quick to accept the Sceptics' arguments. He abandons in effect the kind of knowledge whose truth is in question, our knowledge of things exterior to us, so as to defend the possibility of true knowledge in another form, the unmediated co-presence of the knower and the known in divine intellect. His move looks more like a retreat in the face of the Sceptic's assault than a counter-attack, since the kind of knowledge whose truth interests us is knowledge of the exterior world. His tactic would be more convincing if he could show that the truth guaranteed by the unity of the knower and the known in divine intellect can serve in some way in our attempts to know things other than ourselves, a possibility to be considered below. From Plotinus' point of view, however, his argument ought to help us see the error of a notion such as that of the Gnostics that the mind guiding the making of the world lives in falsehood and ignorance.

4. The Problem of Self-Knowledge (*Ennead* V. 3 [49]. 1–6)

Yet another problem that leads back to the thesis of the unity of intellect and its object, the Forms, is that concerning self-knowledge. Self-knowledge is a fundamental theme in Greek philosophy, from Socrates, who saw self-knowledge as the starting-point of philosophy, to Aristotle, whose god is self-knowledge in absolute form, and the Stoics, who linked happiness to the ability to know oneself and one's place in nature. In attacking philosophers' claims to know something for certain, the Sceptics also attacked the possibility of self-knowledge. Plotinus comes back to the Sceptics' arguments in one of his last treatises, *Ennead* V. 3 [49], and tries to show how the possibility of self-knowledge can be defended in the light of the thesis of the unity of knower and the known in divine intellect.

The Sceptics' argument against the possibility of self-knowledge might be summarized as follows. If something knows itself, then it knows either as a whole or as a part. If it knows as a whole, then nothing is left in it to be the object known. And if it knows as a part, then one part of it knows another part of it. But this is not self-knowledge. Therefore self-knowledge is impossible. However this argument, Plotinus finds (V. 3. 1), leaves open an option. It does not apply to the case of self-knowledge in something that is not composite, that is not a whole made up of parts. But how could there be self-knowledge in such a thing?

In V. 3. 2–4 Plotinus discusses the ways in which our soul knows. It knows (or, rather, seeks to know) things other than itself, this by means of sense-perception and thinking in which perceptual images are compared and judged in relation to various criteria or standards, for example the concept of goodness in relation to which we say something is or is not good. We, as soul, do not know ourselves; we know what is other than us, perceptual images of exterior objects and conceptual standards which we recognize as coming to us from elsewhere (we do not invent them), that is, from an intellect in complete activity which is the source of these standards and which thinks them as the Forms. Thus, in discovering the origin of our knowledge we reach a sort of secondary, derivative awareness of ourselves.

True self-knowledge is found, however, only in the intellect that thinks itself (V. 3. 5–9), in the self-presence of knower and known that it is, in which no spatial distance, no mediating image or representation, no separation between knower and the known intervene so as to turn self-knowledge into an unreliable, unverifiable knowledge of something else:

All will be at the same time one: intellect, intellection, the object of intellection. If therefore its [i.e. intellect's] intellection is the object of intellection, and this object is [intellect], intellect will then think itself. For it will think with intellection, which it is, and think its object, which it is. So in both respects it will think itself, in so far as the intellection is itself and in so far as the object of intellection is itself, which it thinks with intellection, which is itself. (V. 3. 5. 43–8)

Plotinus wishes in general to describe a form of knowledge which is very different from that with which we are familiar. He speaks of it essentially by negating what characterizes the way we know and that makes this knowing so uncertain: typically we know what is other than ourselves as knowers; we depend on mediating images and representations; we must go through long logical processes, deliberations, calculations, arguments, deductions. But these efforts convey an awareness that our attempts to know presuppose the existence of an intellect from which we derive our concepts, which itself possesses these concepts, not as derived (i.e. received or deduced), not as other than itself, but as one with it.

These reflections suggest the following conclusions. What we know (very imperfectly) of what is exterior to us is an externalized, deficient form of self-knowledge. In seeking to know things around us, we indirectly seek to know ourselves. What we know of exterior things is true to the extent that it derives and leads back to the absolute truth of self-knowledge. Self-knowledge is found only in the divine intellect which is one with its object of thought. To know ourselves fully, then, we must become one with the divine intellect.

These conclusions require a good deal more explanation and we will return to them in the following chapters. One problem to be discussed in the next chapter is the following: if true knowledge (which is also self-knowledge) is found only in the unity of the knower and the known in the divine intellect, does this not amount to eliminating knowledge altogether? Does not the concept of knowledge necessarily include a distinction between the knower and the known? If the knower and the known are the same, can we still speak in this case of 'knowledge'? In Chapter 4 the sense in which the knower and the known are the same and yet are different will be examined further.

Looking back at what has been covered in this chapter, one might be tempted to compare Plotinus' approach to Aristotle's. Aristotle was brought by his analysis of the physical world to postulate the existence of an independent immaterial intellect, even though this goes against his strong emphasis on material reality and his insistence on sense-perception as the indispensable vehicle of knowledge. Furthermore he came to the conclusion that his divine intellect can think only of itself; it is a 'thinking of thinking'. Strange as this conclusion may be, it is one entailed by the logic of his theory. Plotinus too finds himself required to postulate, over and beyond the soul that organizes the world, an independent intellect, but an intellect which must be one with the wisdom, the models or Forms which inspire soul in its making of the world.

The claim that the divine intellect is one with its object of thought, the Forms, may strike us as extremely difficult. It is none the less a conclusion to which we must come, not only in trying to explain the order of the world, but also in dealing with the Sceptic attack on the possibility of knowing anything. If we have difficulty with this claim, it is presumably because it postulates a kind of knowledge quite different from the ways of thinking to which we are accustomed, a knowledge which we can only indicate by negating the imperfections of which we are aware in our ways of (more or less) knowing things. Here again Plotinus requires us to leave aside old habits of thought, not only those which interpret everything in corporeal terms, but also those which represent thinking as exclusively 'discursive', that is, as a long-drawn-out process of calculation concerning data relating to exterior objects. However difficult it may be for us to grasp what the perfect knowledge of divine intellect might be like, there is in Plotinus' view no unbridgeable gap between it and our habitual discursive form of thought: since divine intellect constitutes soul it is always present to soul and thus to our souls (see below, Ch. 6); we always remain in contact with it and we can reach it through the deepening of our insight (see below, Ch. 10).

One might be tempted to compare the higher 'non-discursive' way of knowing that Plotinus has in mind with modern concepts of intuitive, artistic, or poetic understanding, as opposed to scientific or logical thought. This comparison could be misleading. Plotinus is not speaking of a form of knowing that is an alternative, possibly a corrective, to science and logic. Rather it represents the goal of science and logic. In his view, discursive thinking is, for us, the means to an end, complete knowledge, and not the end itself, which is a possession of truth such that it is free of the troublesome, fallible methods which we must use to reach it. And this truth is found in the unity constituted by divine intellect and its objects of thought, the Forms.

4

Intellect and the One

1. The Priority of the Simple

Throughout the history of philosophy and science can be found the idea that everything made up of parts, every composite thing, depends and derives in some way from what is not composite, what is simple. This idea might be called the 'Principle of Prior Simplicity'. The Principle of Prior Simplicity has not lost its appeal: it still inspires scientists in their efforts to reconstruct the generation of the elements from an earlier, simpler state of the universe, and similar explanatory patterns, deriving the complex from what is less complex, can be observed, for example, in biology.

The Principle of Prior Simplicity has an important place in Plotinus' philosophy. Indeed he applies it with a rigour such that his overall view of reality is profoundly marked by it and this view as a consequence differs in significant ways from the views of his predecessors. The search for the factors responsible for the constitution of the world had led him to speak, like the Stoics, of a psychic force organizing everything. This force is guided by models: it is inspired by a wisdom which it receives from a divine intellect whose sole activity, its thinking, is this wisdom. Here Plotinus remains close to the positions of some of his Platonist predecessors, notably Alcinous. If Aristotelian philosophers rejected the introduction of the Forms into the divine intellect, they, like Alcinous, regarded divine intellect as the ultimate cause presupposed by the world. For Plotinus, however, divine intellect could not be absolutely simple; in certain respects, despite its high degree of unity, it is composite. Applying the Principle of Prior Simplicity,

Plotinus thus came to the conclusion that we must postulate, over and beyond divine intellect, an ultimate cause which would be absolutely simple, the 'One'. In drawing this conclusion Plotinus not only separated himself from his Platonist and Aristotelian predecessors; he also believed himself to be in a position to throw light on some crucial but obscure passages in Plato's dialogues.

The Principle of Prior Simplicity can mean different things to different philosophers. Our first task then will be to see in what way Plotinus understands the principle and the reasons he has for regarding it as valid. A second matter, to be discussed below in section 2, is Plotinus' claim that divine intellect is not absolutely simple and therefore, by application of the Principle of Prior Simplicity, presupposes a prior cause. This claim is surprising in view of Plotinus' frequent insistence, examined above in Chapter 3, that divine intellect is one with its object of thought, a unity which represented for Alcinous and Aristotelian philosophers an absolute simplicity.

Plotinus formulates the Principle of Prior Simplicity for example in V. 4 [7]. 1. 5–15:

> For there must be something prior to all things which is simple, and this must be different from all that comes after it, being by itself, not mixed with those that come from it, and yet being able to be present in the others in a different way, being truly one, and not something else which is then one. . . .
> For what is not first is in need of what is prior to it, and what is not simple is in need of those which are simple in it so that it may be from them.

It seems obvious enough that something made up of a number of constituent parts, components, or elements comes from them. However, this text shows that the Principle of Prior Simplicity in Plotinus involves more. It includes (1) the thesis that the elements constitutive of compounds exist also independently of these compounds and are different from them, and (2) the thesis that the analysis of compounds into their elements leads back eventually to *one* ultimate element which is absolutely simple and independent of all that derives from it.

The first thesis can be clarified further if we turn to *Ennead.* V. 6 [24]. 3–4. Plotinus is speaking of the One, the ultimate simple:

But it must be single, if it is to be seen in others. Unless one were to say that it has its existence by being with the others. But then it will not be simple, nor will what is made up of many parts exist. For what is not capable of being simple will not exist, and if there is no simple, what is made up of many parts will not exist. (V. 6. 3. 10–15)

Plotinus points to a distinction between elements which exist only as components of a whole (they depend on their status as parts of a whole in order to exist) and elements which make up a whole, existing both as parts of the whole and as independent of the whole. It is the latter type of element that is relevant to the Principle of Prior Simplicity. This element leads a double life, both in a whole, as part of it, and outside the whole, as in itself; it is both immanent in a compound and transcends it. This dual status is common in Plotinus' universe: soul is both part of (in) the world and separate from it; intellect is both part of (in) soul and above it; and the nature of intellect is such that it derives from something which both composes it and is prior to it, the One. This is no universe where immanence excludes transcendence. Plotinus would not accept a view that would force us to choose between a god that is part of the world and a god that is separate from it: god is both.

Let us take up the second thesis included in Plotinus' version of the Principle of Prior Simplicity. According to this thesis, the analysis of compounds into their component parts leads back eventually to one single ultimate element which is absolutely simple and is presupposed, directly or indirectly, by all composite things. Plotinus on the whole takes this thesis for granted, even though one could easily suppose that the analysis of compounds into their component parts leads to an increasing (rather than a decreasing) number of elements (compound A is made up of x number of parts, each part being made up of y number of elements, etc.). In order to understand better Plotinus' assumptions here, it will be useful to consider briefly the Principle of Prior Simplicity as it appears in Plotinus' predecessors.

In a sense the principle is implied already in the efforts of Presocratic philosophers to find a material out of which to derive the manifold world. Nearer to Plotinus is Aristotle's god whose absolute simplicity (it contains no duality of form and matter, potentiality and activity) constitutes the perfection of activity on which depend all changes in the world. Closer yet to Plotinus is Plato, the Plato on whom Aristotle reports in *Metaphysics*, 1. 6, for example, a Plato who held that the Forms (identified as numbers) derive from two prior elements, the 'one' (some formal principle of limitation, it appears) and the 'indefinite dyad' (some material principle, as Aristotle sees it, which is limited by the one). Commenting on Aristotle's text, Alexander of Aphrodisias tells us:

Plato and the Pythagoreans thought that the numbers were the cause of being, for they took the first and non-composite as cause, surfaces being first in relation to bodies, being more simple and independent in their being of body, lines being first in relation to surfaces, and points are first in relation to lines, being totally non-composite and having nothing prior to them.[1]

According to this text, Plato saw the production of reality as a kind of mathematical progression, in which the point is an element of, and produces, the line, just as the line is an element of, and produces, the surface, which in turn produces a solid (see figure). In this way all of reality derives from two ultimate elements, the 'one' and the 'dyad'.

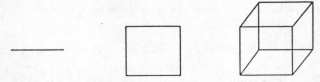

Much is (and will remain) obscure in these and other Aristotelian reports on Plato: What precisely is meant by the 'one' and the 'dyad'? How exactly do they produce the Forms? Some modern scholars regard such Aristotelian texts as little more than gross misunderstandings of certain passages in Plato's dialogues. Others think the reports go back to an esoteric 'oral teaching' given by Plato in the Academy. Plotinus, at any rate, accepts such reports as true and does not hesitate to cite them, for example at V. 4 [7]. 2. 8–9.

[1] Alexander of Aphrodisias, *On Aristotle's Metaphysics*, ed. M. Hayduck (Berlin, 1891), 55. 20–6 (p. 84 of W. Dooley's translation (London, 1989)).

Nor is he the first to be influenced by the Aristotelian reports on Plato. Alcinous already described his first cause as follows: 'The supreme god is without parts, for nothing is prior to him; for the part and what constitutes a compound is prior to the compound of which it is a part. For the surface is prior to the body and the line is prior to the surface' (*Didaskalikos*, ch. 10). Texts such as this show how Plotinus would have been led to accept the Principle of Prior Simplicity, in the version represented, as authentically Platonic. And this version, in particular in its use of a mathematical series, entails the reduction of the manifold world to an ever-decreasing number of elements.

It could be objected at this point that if it is the case that complex mathematical entities such as surfaces can be derived from one single element, the point, just as larger numbers can be derived from a first unit, the number 1, this might not be the case outside mathematics, in relation to other sorts of things:

For prior to the many the one is needed, from which come the many. For in the realm of number the one is first. But they speak like this of number, for the numbers that follow [the one] are composed. Yet why must this be true of beings, so that among them there is a one from which the many come? [If this were not the case] then the many would be scattered and apart from each other, each coming by chance to the composite from different places. (V. 3 [49]. 12. 9–14)

Plotinus argues that the various compounds that are found in reality (plants, animals, the world, soul, intellect) are not arbitrary aggregates of prior elements: they are organized, unified structures. The elements that constitute them must give them unity (e.g. soul constitutes and unifies the world). And the series of unifying elements must end with an ultimate single element which is the source of unity in all else. This argument is developed at greater length at the beginning of VI. 9 [9], where Plotinus takes up the (Stoic) idea that compound things in the world (houses, plants, animals, etc.) represent different degrees of intensity of unification. The fact that each compound is a kind of unity is understood as pointing to a source of unity which itself, if it is a unified compound, presupposes a further source of unity. The series can only end with a source of unity which is both absolutely non-composite and the *single* source of the unity of everything.

The Principle of Prior Simplicity, in the form it takes in Plotinus, includes finally a third thesis, a thesis which shows the distance between Plotinus' version of the principle and modern versions: for him the element which is prior to a compound is also superior to the compound in power and being. It is superior in power because it produces the compound. And it is superior in being because it exists at a higher level of perfection: it possesses unity, self-integrity, independence to a greater degree. Thus soul is superior to body and intellect to soul. And thus the One, as the absolute simple presupposed by intellect, must be superior to intellect.

2. Divine Intellect as Composite

The need to go beyond divine intellect in the search for the ultimate cause of reality derives from the Principle of Prior Simplicity as applied to the claim that divine intellect is composite. This claim is crucial. With it Plotinus separates himself from Platonists and Aristotelians who held that the unity of divine intellect and its object of thought is such that it is absolutely simple and therefore ultimate. Plotinus' position is not made easier by his insistence in other contexts on the unity composed by intellect and its object.

Arguments showing that divine intellect is composite can be found, for example, in *Ennead* V. 4 and V. 6. V. 4. 2 suggests that divine intellect is composite in two ways: (1) it is a compound of the act and of the object of thinking; the act of thinking (*noesis*) and the object that defines this act (*noeton*) make up intellect (*nous*); (2) the object itself is multiple.

1. To appreciate the first point, we must recall very briefly Aristotle's analysis of the process of thinking in *De anima*, 3. 4–6, since this analysis is Plotinus' starting-point. According to Aristotle, a certain kind of potential, the potential to think, is brought to activity by being defined by, or by receiving, certain forms (we could call them concepts) that are the realization of this potential. The

potential is immaterial, as are the forms it receives, and together they become one. This helps us see how Aristotle's divine intellect, in thinking itself, is one with its object of thought, that is, absolutely simple.

However Plotinus, in V. 6. 1–2, claims that the (Aristotelian) analysis of thinking implies on the contrary that all thinking, including self-thought, involves necessarily a duality of thinking and of object of thought. This is so because the constitution of intellect depends on the prior existence of the object of thought so as to make possible the actualization of the potential to think. Thus the object of thought exists both in intellect, as a constitutive component, and before it, as that in relation to which thought is realized. If then intellect thinks itself, it is both single, as thinking *itself*, and dual, as *thinking* something. All thought, including self-thought, is constituted through a duality of act and of the object of thinking, and the object, as constitutive of thought, must exist prior to thought as well as in thought. In Plotinus' mind Aristotle's analysis of thinking leads to the conclusion that the Aristotelian god, as self-thought, cannot be what it claims to be, absolutely simple and ultimate.

Broader, less technical considerations are proposed a little later in V. 6. Plotinus places thinking in a wider context: 'And this is thinking, a movement to what is good, desiring it. For the desire generated thinking and produced it with itself. For seeing is the desire of sight' (V. 6. 5. 8–10). Thinking is essentially an act directed to something else, something it lacks. Thinking implies deficiency: it reaches toward, and therefore cannot be, absolute self-sufficiency: 'And again knowledge is a certain yearning and as if a finding by him who sought' (V. 3 [49]. 10. 49–50).

2. Another way in which divine intellect shows itself to be composite is in the multiplicity characterizing its object of thought. Plotinus believes of course that divine intellect thinks the Forms and that the Forms are manifold. The differences between the Forms might be reason enough for Platonists to agree that divine intellect, in thinking the Forms, cannot be absolutely simple. However such an argument would not convince Aristotelians, and they are, in part at least, the opponents Plotinus has in mind in his effort to show that the divine intellect is not simple.

Aristotelians might be more convinced by a line of reflection developed in *Ennead* V. 3 [49]. 10. Here Plotinus makes the point that all thinking implies variety, differences, in what is thought. This is illustrated on the level of language:

> For if [intellect] were to direct its attention to an object which is one and without parts, it could say nothing. For what would it have to say about it, or what could it understand? For if what is altogether without parts needed to say itself, it must first say the things that it is not, so that in this way it would be many, so as to be one. Then whenever it would say 'I am this', if the 'this' it says is different from itself, then it will be telling falsehood. If it says something accidental to itself, it will say many things or will say this, 'am am' and 'I I'. What then if it were merely two and said 'I and this'? But then it must already be many, and indeed as different things, and where there are different things there is already number and much else. What thinks must therefore take different things, and what is thought, as being thought, must be varied, or there will not be thought of it, but a touching and so to speak an ineffable and unintelligible contact. (V. 3. 10. 31–43)

Just as there is no speech without differences and multiplicity in what is said, so thought is possible only if its object is differentiated, varied, multiple.

In conclusion, divine intellect must be, as intellect, both a duality (of thinking and object thought) and a multiplicity (as object of thought). In both cases intellect is composite. The search for the ultimate cause, as this cause is required by the Principle of Prior Simplicity, must go beyond intellect, postulating a reality which is absolutely simple, which both constitutes intellect and is different from and independent of intellect.

This result is established with such clarity and strength that it poses a serious challenge for Aristotelian metaphysics. Plotinus also undermines the position of those among his Platonist predecessors such as Numenius and Alcinous who identified the ultimate cause as divine intellect. And their position is put in question in yet another respect. Like their Aristotelian contemporaries, these Platonists did not think of divine intellect as the *only* ultimate or first cause: reality was constituted through the combination of a number of first causes, divine intellect, world-soul, matter. Strict adherence to the Principle of Prior Simplicity requires however, in Plotinus' view, the conclusion that there can be but *one* ultimate cause, one single source of all reality.

The far-reaching consequences of this conclusion will be examined below in Chapters 6 and 7. We should note here that Plotinus' radical monism—his claim that all reality derives from a single cause—appears to have been anticipated by some Platonist and Pythagorean philosophers of the first centuries BC and AD. Using concepts such as those attributed to Plato by Aristotle and the Aristotelian commentators, these philosophers appear to have spoken of the 'dyad' as coming from the 'one', whereas the Aristotelian reports on Plato give the impression that for Plato the 'one' and the 'dyad' acted as two first causes. What little we know about these philosophers shows however no trace of the rigorous thinking whereby Plotinus reached his conclusions.

Plotinus found that his position matches Plato's rare and enigmatic indications about the ultimate cause of reality. In the *Republic* Plato writes (509b) about a 'Form of the Good' that is 'beyond being in power and dignity', being the source of the existence of the Forms and of knowledge. Plotinus is now in a position, he feels, to explain this text. The 'Form of the Good' is in fact the ultimate simple, the One. It is 'beyond being' in that it is different from, as prior to, the unity of intellect and the Forms that are 'true being'. (Plotinus' interpretation underplays the fact that Plato refers to 'the Good' as a *Form*.) And the Good is the source of the Forms and of knowledge in the sense that it is the ultimate constitutive element of divine intellect and its object, the Forms. Furthermore this ultimate cause corresponds to the 'one' of which Aristotle speaks in his reports on Plato. Finally the ultimate cause as identified by Plotinus matches the 'one' which Plato discusses in the second part of the *Parmenides* (137c–142a). In reading this part of the *Parmenides* as if it propounded metaphysical doctrine (as opposed to the obscure logical exercises that are usually found in this text today), Plotinus was anticipated by some of the monistic predecessors mentioned above. In his case, however, this interpretation fits into a well-developed and argued theory of ultimate causation.

Plotinus' reasoning brings new difficulties. In the next chapter one of these will be explored: if the One is 'beyond being' and beyond intellect, how is it possible for us to think and speak of it? A further difficulty is presented by the fact that Plato, in Aristotle's reports, speaks of another ultimate cause besides the 'one', the 'indefinite dyad': how can this be reconciled with Plotinus' conviction that there is only one ultimate source of reality? This question will be examined in Chapter 6, in the context of a larger problem, that concerning the manner in which manifold reality derives from something absolutely simple.

5

Speaking of the One

1. The Ineffability of the One (*Ennead* VI. 9 [9]. 3)

The argument Plotinus follows in postulating an ultimate cause of all things, an absolutely simple reality, different from and superior to divine intellect, leads also to the conclusion that this cause must lie beyond the realm of knowledge and discourse: the One is unknowable and ineffable. In this chapter the ineffability of the One will be examined, in particular as regards the paradox that the One, if ineffable, is nevertheless spoken about. In the next chapter the unknowability of the One will be discussed in connection with the emergence of divine intellect as a knowing of the unknowable.

It was common enough in Plotinus' time to say that the highest cause, or god, was unknowable and ineffable. Platonists could refer in this regard to a number of passages in Plato's works. In the *Timaeus* (28c) Plato says that the divine artisan or demiurge of the world is difficult to discover and impossible to communicate to all men. In the *Republic* (509b) the Form of the Good is said to be 'beyond being'; but being is what is knowable.[1] The *Parmenides* (142c) states that there is no name for the 'one'. And the *Seventh Letter* (whose authenticity was not questioned at the time) claims that the object of Plato's research cannot be spoken (341c). These texts prompted Platonists such as Alcinous (*Didaskalikos*, ch. 10) to deny that anything could be said of the ultimate cause: it is ineffable. At the same time, however, they did not hesitate to ascribe various characteristics to the first cause, saying for example that it is an intellect.

---

[1] However, in referring to the Good as a Form, Plato seems to think of the Good as an object of knowledge.

This suggests some confusion about what is meant by the claim that the first cause is ineffable. Is it ineffable merely in the sense that it is just *difficult* to know and describe, not being immediately accessible? Or is it the case that the first cause is such that it *cannot* be known or spoken? Plotinus' predecessors do not seem to have worked out a clear position on this. This is hardly surprising, since they are already unclear about how to answer questions dealing with the metaphysical status of the first cause: Is it a divine intellect? If so, how can it be 'beyond being', as Plato's *Republic* suggests? What does 'beyond being' mean?

Plotinus is quite clear that the One is unknowable and ineffable in the sense that it cannot function as an object of knowledge and discourse. This is so because of what is entailed by the One's status as the absolutely simple element presupposed by divine intellect. As such the One must be prior to (or 'above') all determinate being:

> For intellect is something, one of the beings, but it [the One] is not some thing, but is prior to each, nor is it a being. For being has, as it were, the shape of being, but it is without shape and intelligible form. For as generating all things, the nature of the One is none of them. Nor is it something, or a quality or quantity or intellect or soul. Nor does it move or rest. Nor is it in place or time, but is 'itself by itself uniform' [*Symposium*, 211b] or rather without form and prior to all form, prior to movement and rest. For these have to do with being, making it many. (VI. 9. 3. 36–45)

The One is thus not a 'thing', not something with a form, with a determinate or finite character. In this sense it is infinite. However knowledge can only have for its object something which is determinate and manifold (see above, Ch. 4 s. 2). Yet the One, as prior to intellect and being, is neither. It cannot therefore be known. And as speech, Plotinus believes (see I. 2. 3. 27–31), is an expression of thought, so the absolutely unknowable cannot be spoken.

In a later text, VI. 8 [39]. 8, Plotinus provides a further reason for claiming that the One is ineffable. Discussing whether 'liberty' or 'necessity' might be attributed to the One, Plotinus points out that the expression 'liberty' refers to a complex situation, the relation of one thing to another. It concerns the manifold reality familiar to us and not that which is prior to this reality. We could generalize this point by saying that our language relates to the varied world in which we live; it cannot apply to what is presupposed by and other than this world.

2. Speaking about the One (*Enneads* VI. 9. 3–4, V. 3 [49]. 14)

Plotinus thus arrives at a position concerning the ineffability of the first cause which is clearer than what we find in his predecessors. He is also keenly aware of the dilemma in which he finds himself. For the ineffability of the One is asserted in a context in which much is said about the One. Is such discourse self-contradictory? How could anything be said about the unsayable? Plotinus formulates the dilemma in this way:

> How do we then speak about it? We say something about it, but we do not say it, nor do we have knowledge or thought of it. How then do we speak about it, if we do not have it? Or, if we do not possess it by means of knowledge, do we not have it at all? But we have it in such a way as to speak about it, but not to say it itself. (V. 3. 14. 1–6)

According to Plotinus, then, we cannot speak the One, since it is ineffable, but we can in some sense speak 'about' it. But how is this possible?

An answer can be found already in VI. 9, in chapter 3, where the ineffability of the One is so clearly formulated:

> Since to say it [the One] is the cause is to predicate an attribute not of it, but of us, in that we have something from it, [it] which exists in itself. But he who speaks accurately should not say 'it' or 'exists', but we circle around it on the outside, as it were, wishing to communicate our impressions, sometimes coming near, sometimes falling back on account of the dilemmas that surround it. (VI. 9. 3. 49–55)

When we speak 'about' the One, saying it is the cause, we are in fact speaking of ourselves, saying that we are causally dependent and expressing what we experience in this condition of dependence. We are speaking of ourselves when we speak about the One. In this way the One remains ineffable in itself, even though we speak about it.

Examples can be found in VI. 9, chapters 5 and 6, of how what is said of the One may be interpreted as referring in fact to what depends on it. To speak of the first cause as 'the One' is inappropriate, if by this we mean to describe it (5. 30–46). The term 'one' refers primarily to such things as the geometrical point or the arithmetical unit. We adapt these concepts in seeking to bring our souls and thoughts to greater unity, in elaborating a notion of what overcomes our dispersion into multiplicity. Similarly, the One cannot be described as being in itself 'good'. The word 'good' is relative: it refers to a deficiency in something in some respect (what is good *for* it). It follows that the absolute first cause, being totally self-sufficient and needing nothing, is not of itself good. When we speak of 'the Good', we are indicating our own needs, our own lack of self-sufficiency in relation to what might ultimately satisfy us (6. 34–42).

In V. 3. 14 Plotinus finds a striking image of what he means when he says that, in speaking about the One, we are speaking, not of it, but of our own nature and experiences:

But we have it in such a way as to speak about it, but not to say it itself. And we say what it is not; what it is, we do not say. So that it is from what is posterior [to it] that we speak about it. We are not hindered from having it, although we do not say it. But like those who are inspired and become [divinely] possessed, if they manage to know that they have something greater in themselves, even if they do not know what, from that through which they are moved and speak, from this they acquire a sense of the mover, being different from it, thus do we appear to relate to it [the One]. (V. 3. 14. 5–14)

The dependence that we experience in us and in the things around us is the presence of the One in us and in the world, and it is of this that we speak when we speak about the One.

3. A Dilemma Resolved?

The ideas examined above suggest that Plotinus succeeded in avoiding the self-contradiction of claiming that the One is ineffable while affirming various things of the One. He is clear that, when we speak about the One, we should do so in a manner that preserves its ineffability. He explains how this is possible by suggesting that talk of the One is talk 'about' it, that is, talk of ourselves and of other aspects of the world (which *can* be spoken) as manifesting a dependence, deficiency, or need in relation to something prior to them or higher than them.

If indeed this approach is successful in maintaining the ineffability of the One, does it achieve this, one might wonder, by paying too high a price? If, in speaking of the One, we are in fact speaking of what comes after it, then in what sense are we still really speaking about the One? If by speaking of the One as the Good, I am in fact saying that I am lacking in some respect, am I not simply speaking about *myself*? How can I distinguish between speaking about myself and speaking about myself as a way of speaking about the One? Does not fidelity to the principle of ineffability drive us to abandoning all speech, of whatever sort, about the One?

It seems reasonable to expect Plotinus to be able to distinguish between speaking of things and speaking of things as a way of speaking about the One. Otherwise he is faced with confusion, in particular the loss of the distinction between the One and what it produces. It is true that the importance of the One, as the founding principle of reality, is such that it is everywhere present in things as constituting them. And it is true that Plotinus' discourse is largely directed to bringing us to the discovery of the One and to union with it (see below, Ch. 10). Yet some distinction still seems necessary between speaking of things and speaking of the One.

An approach to dealing with this difficulty might involve the following steps. We might argue that speaking of things as a way of speaking about the One is specifically about the One to the extent that it singles out in particular the dependence, deficiency, or need in things. In speaking in this way we are saying that neither we nor the things around us are ultimate and self-sufficient. Using Plotinus' image of people possessed by a god, we can say that our dependence on something beyond us is the presence of this in us and it is of this presence that we speak when we speak about the One. This is sufficient to allow us to distinguish between speaking of things and speaking of things as a way of speaking about the One.

One might add that this speaking takes place in a particular context, for instance in the words of Plotinus' treatises, words directed to the reader who wishes to understand the world and attain the good. Plotinus' words about the One are not gratuitous mind-games; their purpose is to lead the reader to insight into the world, human nature, and their origin. In this situation the reader is far from the end of his philosophical journey, a direct grasp of the One. Rather the reader is at the beginning, moving towards a first notion of the non-ultimacy of the things that are most familiar. At higher stages in the journey, when greater knowledge is attained, words, as the expression and communication of knowledge, are no longer necessary; they give way to the silence that is the grasp of truth in the divine intellect, a silence which is a preparation for union with the One. Thus all speech, including speech about the One, takes place for the use of souls which have not yet reached the knowledge that will lead them to union with the One. It is therefore appropriate that speech about the One refers to the things that are at first most familiar to us, in so far as they point beyond themselves.

6

The Derivation of All Things
from the One (I)

1. The Question of Derivation

The analysis of the world that begins with the discovery of soul as
the force responsible for organizing things leads to the conclusion
that soul presupposes a divine intellect as the source of the wisdom
guiding it. This divine intellect, thought by Aristotelians and by
some Platonists to be ultimate, is shown by Plotinus to presuppose a
further principle which constitutes it, the One. If we follow this
reasoning leading us 'up' from the world to its first cause, we can also
follow a line of enquiry going in the opposite direction, leading us
'down' from the One to the world that derives from it. In following
this second path, in this and in the following chapter, we will be able
to examine matters from a new point of view, adding to what has
already been said about the relations between the One and intellect,
between intellect and soul, between the various kinds of soul, and
between them and the world.

In this chapter the constitution of things by the One will be
referred to as a process of 'derivation'. The word 'derivation',
understood literally, has associations with the flowing of water.
These associations are stronger in the case of another term
frequently used in connection with Plotinus, 'emanation'. Plotinus
himself uses images of water or light 'emanating' (flowing) from a
source in order to describe things coming from the One. However,
he is well aware that emanation is a material process which cannot
properly be attributed to immaterial entities: emanation may

function as an image of processes that occur at higher levels of being; it is not itself these processes (see III. 4 [15]. 3. 25–7). To avoid the misleading connotations of the word emanation I shall use the somewhat less specific term 'derivation'. One could also speak of the 'creation' or 'making' of things by the One. However, 'creation' might bring with it Christian ideas not relevant to Plotinus, and 'making' (a term which suggests a comparison with artisanal fabrication) involves, as we will see (below, Ch. 7), other problems. What matters is the process to be designated by these terms: what precisely does the constitution of things by the One involve?

In a number of passages Plotinus describes derivation as one of the major traditional problems of philosophy:

But [soul] desires [a solution] to the problem which is so often discussed, even by the ancient sages, as to how from the One, being such as we say the One is, anything can be constituted, either a multiplicity, a dyad, or a number; [why] it did not stay by itself, but so great a multiplicity flowed out as is seen in what is. (V. 1 [10]. 6. 3–8)

Plotinus is thinking here of the first Greek philosophers who, according to Aristotle, sought to elaborate the world in all its complexity from an original material. He is thinking also of Plato who, again according to Aristotle, derived the Forms and the world from two ultimate principles, the 'one' and the 'indefinite dyad' (see above, Ch. 4 s. 1). However, Plotinus reads Aristotle's report as if it said that for Plato all things (including the 'dyad') derive from the 'one'. We need then to ask *why* Plotinus feels that all things must come from one single source (and not from two or more causes), as well as considering the question which he formulates above concerning *how* they come from this source. And both questions presuppose some account of what Plotinus means when he affirms that things 'come from' the One.

In the passage quoted above Plotinus speaks of things as being 'constituted', or (if we translate more literally) as 'having existence' from the One. To explain what this means we might return to the Principle of Prior Simplicity (above, Ch. 4). This principle postulates elements which constitute compounds while continuing to exist as themselves. Compounds thus depend for their existence on these elements. A compound, if it has an existence proper to it, has it only to the extent that its constitutive elements exist and come together to produce it. In this sense the compound derives from, or has its existence from, its elements. In the version of the Principle of Prior Simplicity applied by Plotinus, the chain of elements and their derivative compounds terminates in one ultimate constitutive element, the One (see above, Ch. 4 s. 1). Thus there must in the final analysis be a single constitutive element from which all else, directly or indirectly, takes its existence.

The Principle of Prior Simplicity enables us in this way to give some content to Plotinus' affirmation that everything comes from the One and we can do this without having recourse to the potentially misleading images of emanation or (artisanal) making. We are also in a position to say why, for him, all must come from a single source.

2. The Derivation of Intellect (*Ennead* V. 4 [7], V. 1 [10]. 6–7)

By insisting that all things come from one ultimate constitutive principle Plotinus has made things a good deal harder for himself than had he allowed for two or more factors whose interreaction might explain the emergence of the world. How could reality, in all its variety, derive from one non-composite element? Plotinus must show how this is possible if he is to keep to his version of the Principle of Prior Simplicity and all that it entails. A further problem Plotinus faces is that everything must derive from the One without implicating the One in any form of change, for such change would mean ending the perfect simplicity that is required of the One as first cause. Aristotle before had found himself in a comparable situation, since his divine intellect was required to move others without itself moving or changing.

Since the One is postulated as the ultimate principle presupposed by divine intellect, it is the derivation of divine intellect from the One which represents the first stage of the coming into existence of things from the One. How does this first stage occur?

We should notice that our question concerns the One and its relation to intellect. Thus we are asking for an answer involving what is in itself unknowable and ineffable. What kind of answer is it appropriate to expect? Using ideas explored above (Ch. 5), we might suppose that the answer will refer to examples of the process of derivation that are more familiar to us and that could be of help in diminishing the difficulties we have in seeing how intellect could come from the One.

One example Plotinus gives in V. 4. 1 is the productivity of living things. Living things, when they reach maturity, the perfection of their nature, normally procreate (1. 25–30). A major theme in Aristotle's biology, this principle extends for Plotinus both down to inorganic things (see the next paragraph) and up to the divine, for the divine, as Plato says (*Timaeus*, 29e), is not envious: it is generous and gives of itself. It seems generally true then that when things reach maturity or perfection they procreate or give of themselves in some way. Since the One represents the highest perfection, how can we say that the productivity of perfection does not occur in its case, insisting that it remain in selfish isolation, giving nothing of itself? Plotinus thus suggests that more familiar cases of productivity make it plausible to think *that* the One gives existence to things. But he does not show *how* this occurs.

He goes somewhat further by observing a general pattern in things that are productive. The cases of fire giving off heat (V. 4. 2. 27–33), the sun giving off light, and snow giving off cold (V. 1. 6. 28–35) are claimed to be examples of a wider pattern: each substance (e.g. fire) has a primary (or internal) activity proper to itself and gives rise to a secondary activity (e.g. heat) external to, or different from, the primary activity. Even if the One is strictly speaking not a thing or a substance (see above, Ch. 5 s. 1), it is plausible that the structure of primary and secondary activities found in lower things applies also in its case and that the absolutely simple activity which it is gives rise to a secondary activity which is different from it.

What is this secondary activity of the One? Plotinus identifies it with the indefinite dyad mentioned in the Aristotelian reports on Plato, but he interprets it as the undefined potentiality which, in Aristotle's theory of thinking, becomes determined or actualized by objects of thought. The object of thought that defines the indeterminate potentiality, making it intellect, is the One. However, the One is not such as to be thinkable, since it is neither determinate nor manifold (above, Ch. 5 s. 1). The dyad which is the One's secondary activity must then 'turn toward' the One and think of it as thinkable, as rendered determinate and manifold. The result is the self-thought that is divine intellect. Divine intellect is a knowing of the unknowable: it knows the One as knowing itself, a determinate manifold expression of the One in the indeterminate potentiality to think that is the One's secondary activity.

Plotinus' account of the derivation of intellect from the One is clearly very difficult and involves many problems of which the following might be mentioned:

1. How does the One's secondary activity emerge from the One? The examples of fire and heat, sun and light, imply processes of emanation, but emanation as a physical process is not relevant to the One. More generally Plotinus does not sufficiently show that the structure of double activity (primary/secondary, internal/external) applies to realities outside the limited realm of such things as fire, nor does he show in what way it applies to such realities.

2. How does the One's secondary activity 'turn toward' the One? What is this 'turning'? The concept of a lower entity turning toward and contemplating a higher being so as to be inspired by it is anticipated in Aristotle's solution to the problem of how divine intellect moves others without moving: it does so as an object of thought and love which inspires imitation in the heavenly bodies (*Metaphysics*, 12. 7). Alcinous adopts this solution (*Didaskalikos*, chs. 10, 14): his first god, a divine intellect, acts by inspiring a lower god to turn toward, contemplate, and imitate it. Plotinus clearly sees the advantage of this approach: it allows the One to be responsible for processes without requiring any change in it. But what precisely is meant by saying that the One's secondary activity 'turns toward' the One?

3. How, in turning toward the One, does the One's secondary activity render the One thinkable, that is, determinate and manifold? The supreme gods of Aristotle and Alcinous are thinkable (as intellects), but Plotinus' One is not. Plotinus seems to have in mind the Pythagorean idea, to be found in Plato (*Philebus*, 16c–17a,

23cd) and Aristotle (*Metaphysics*, 1. 5), of a principle of limit that delimits or articulates what is indeterminate. But how does the One, which is without form or determination, act as a principle of determination?

In examining these problems, some of which are explored by Plotinus himself (for example in VI. 7 [38]. 15–17), we should, I think, keep in mind the restrictions attaching to any attempt to explain the derivation of divine intellect from the One. At most, broad patterns in the productivity of the things that we observe, structures of derivation that we can generalize, may be brought forward in order to show the improbability (in any case invalidated by the fact of the existence of the world) that the One must remain sterile. Its perfection implies on the contrary its productivity. In a curious way, then, the most simple of realities must also be the most powerful since it gives existence to everything. Because as first cause it is not limited by any prior cause its power can even be described as infinite. As for the question of how exactly everything comes from the One, again we must refer to patterns of derivation in lower things, referring in particular as regards the first stage of derivation to the most relevant instance, that of the constitution of thought.

It should be noted finally that the derivation of divine intellect from the One must take place outside time, since time is produced by soul which derives from intellect (below, Ch. 7 s. 3). There can be no beginning or end to the derivation of intellect. It does not happen at a particular moment. To speak of the One as giving rise to divine intellect would be misleading if we were to imagine this as taking place in the framework of time and space, occurring at a moment such as those moments marking lower processes of derivation or production. Divine intellect exists as an eternal, that is extra-temporal, expression of the One.

3. The Derivation of Soul (*Ennead* V. 1. 7, V. 2. 1)

As the One, the element presupposed by divine intellect, is that from which intellect takes its existence or derives, so intellect, as that which is presupposed by soul (above, Ch. 3), constitutes or gives existence to soul. Indeed the process whereby soul derives from intellect repeats that whereby intellect derives from the One, as Plotinus suggests in V. 2. 1. 14–18:

Now [intellect], being like [the One], produces similar effects, pouring out great power—this is a form of it—just as what is prior to it poured forth. And this activity coming from being is of soul, which becomes this while [intellect] stays [the same]. For intellect is also generated without the One changing.

We can thus explain how intellect constitutes soul in much the same way as we have explained how the One constitutes intellect: intellect as perfection is productive; it has a primary (internal) activity accompanied by a secondary activity which by 'turning toward' intellect is defined by it (cf. V. 1. 7. 36–46). Soul is then an expression of intellect, a projection, so to speak, at a further degree of dispersion, of the perfectly unified determinate expression of the One that is divine intellect.

There are some difficulties, however, in seeing the nature of soul simply in terms of its emergence as a product derived from intellect. In particular this emergence does not appear to explain adequately certain characteristics proper to soul. Plotinus says, for example:

It is the work of the more rational soul to think, but not just to think. For what would distinguish it from intellect? But adding something else to [its function of] being rational, it did not stay intellect. It has a [specific] work, as does every part of intelligible being. Looking to what is prior to it, it thinks it, and [looking] to itself, it arranges what comes after it and organizes and rules it, since it was not possible for everything to remain in the intelligible. (IV. 8 [6]. 3. 21–8)

It is characteristic of soul, as already seen above in Chapter 1, to organize what is inferior to it, the material world. Plotinus also finds in soul the ability to be present indivisibly throughout body (IV. 2 [4]. 1, 43–6; IV. 1 [21]. 8–9; above, Ch. 2). These two characteristics of soul—to organize bodies and be present in bodies—define the nature of soul in terms of its relation to the material world. Yet if we follow strictly the order of the derivation of all things, stage by stage, from the One, soul emerges from intellect at a stage *prior* (not in time, but in the order in which things are constituted) to the derivation of the material world from soul. How can body serve to define what is constituted prior to it?

It can be argued in Plotinus' defence that it is possible to use body in defining what exists prior to it, soul, to the extent that body is itself an expression of soul's power and potential (see IV. 8. 3. 24–8). However, it is important to avoid confusing this approach, which sees soul as a stage in the derivation of things from the One, with the more traditional Platonist view according to which soul is defined by being assigned a place within the framework of a pre-established system of two worlds (the material and the immaterial). These two approaches are incompatible in the sense that the pre-established system of two worlds, if it presupposes that the two worlds exist independently of each other and are prior to soul, is not compatible with the theory of the derivation of everything from the One.

A comparable situation arises if we look briefly at the question of the distinction between souls or types of soul. Plotinus thinks of soul, as a product of intellect, as both one soul and a multiplicity of souls. But what makes the difference between these souls? He distinguishes between soul as an intelligible reality, the soul governing the world (world-soul), and the souls present in individual bodies. It seems evident that what differentiates these souls is their different relationships to body and to different bodies (the body of the world, individual bodies). The differences between soul, world-soul, and individual souls make best sense in relation to differences in their relationships to body: body is what produces the distinctions between souls. However, Plotinus rejects this (see IV. 3 [27]. 2): he claims that souls are different from each other independently of, and prior to, their presence in bodies, as part of their constitution as an expression of divine intellect; as intellect is one and many, a unity of thought and its object which is also a multiplicity of Forms (themselves intellects), so intellect's immediate expression, soul, is a corresponding unity and multiplicity of souls.

A meticulous and open-minded examination of this subject[1] has not found that such questions concerning Plotinus' theory of soul are

---

[1] See H. Blumenthal, 'Soul, World-Soul, Individual Soul', in *Le Néoplatonisme* (Paris, 1971), 56–63.

easily resolved. At least one source of difficulty, I believe, is the presence in Plotinus' thinking of two different world-views: the view, inherited from his Platonist predecessors, that reality is made up of two independently existing levels of reality (the world of Forms and a realm of disorganized matter) which are linked by soul (which organizes matter according to the Forms); and his new theory of derivation according to which soul does not bring together independently existing things, but is the product of one (intellect) and produces the other (the material world). The presence of these two views will be noticed again at the beginning of Chapter 7.

4. Does the One Produce of Necessity? (*Ennead* VI. 8 [39])

Before examining in the next chapter the following stage of derivation, the generation of the material world by soul, it may be useful to consider briefly the question whether the One produces reality of necessity or freely. This question derives principally from religious criticisms of Plotinus in which it is claimed that the necessity whereby Plotinus' One generates things compares (unfavourably) with the free act of love whereby God creates.

The belief that this comparison is valid rests primarily, it would seem, on literal interpretations of Plotinus' images of emanation. According to these readings the One in Plotinus generates with the same automatic necessity that a fountain produces water. However, a more exact appreciation of Plotinus' use of images of emanation ought to cast doubt on this. In any case Plotinus devoted one of his finest treatises, *Ennead* VI. 8 [39], to the subject of freedom and necessity in the One, a treatise which the interested reader ought not to have any difficulty in finding in view of the title which it is given by Porphyry, *On Free Will and the Will of the One*. This work does not lend itself to the simplifications of theological polemic and has much to offer to those who are concerned with the philosophical issues at stake.

Rather than attempting to survey the contents of VI. 8, it might be appropriate to mention here some of the important points made by Plotinus which could be explored further (along with much else) in a careful reading of the treatise. One should note first that in this context the contrasting concepts of necessity and freedom refer primarily to the human situation in the world. If one wishes to avoid crude anthropomorphism, one ought to ask how these concepts can be used (if at all) of realities that transcend the human condition. In a sense the contrast of freedom and necessity cannot be appropriately applied to what transcends our experience. While emphasizing the absolute transcendence of the One and its ineffability, Plotinus also shows how the analysis of human freedom, when extended upwards in the direction of the One, involves a decrease of restrictions on freedom such that absolute freedom is reached when the level of the One is reached. Plotinus relates freedom to that which is in our control, as opposed to external constraints imposed on us. These constraints include corporeal passions, whereas control derives from independence of judgement. As this judgement must operate with knowledge, not ignorance, it is found in its most unrestricted form in divine intellect. Yet intellect is not absolutely free in the sense that it relates to another, the Good beyond it, the One, which is beyond all constraint, external limitation, or directedness to another. The One may thus be said to will both itself and what it produces with absolute freedom (see chs. 13, 18). As the source of intellect and all else it may also be said to be the source and basis of the qualified forms of freedom in others. In elaborating and discussing these Plotinian ideas we should keep in mind the One's ineffability and the fact that we are attempting to conceive of what lies beyond the limitations and constraints on freedom in which we live (see ch. 8).

7

The Derivation of All Things
from the One (II)

1. The Making of the World in Plato's *Timaeus*

What is the origin of this world in which we live? This has been the
principal question pursued in the preceding chapters. The identification of certain causes (soul, intellect, the One) presupposed by the
world can hardly satisfy completely as an answer to the question. We
also need to see how the world is constituted (or derives) from these
causes. For Platonists the key text concerning this subject is Plato's
Timaeus, a wonderful but in many respects puzzling account of the
genesis of the world. Some of the problems posed by the
interpretation of the *Timaeus* need to be considered before approaching Plotinus' discussion of the constitution of the world.

Timaeus, the main figure in Plato's dialogue, tells a 'probable tale'
(*Timaeus*, 29d) about the generation of the world, a tale which makes
use of various images, in particular that of artisanal making. As the
human artisan (or craftsman) produces an object by taking an
appropriate material, wood for example, and shaping this material
according to the design or model that he has in mind, so there is a
divine craftsman (the 'demiurge') who uses a model (the eternal
Forms) which he imitates, producing in some kind of medium
(described as the 'receptacle') an imitation which is the world
(*Timaeus*, 28a–29d).

Taking this account literally, Aristotle attacked it. Is it not absurd
to think of nature as labouring like a craftsman who must plot,
calculate, and worry, toiling with what material lies to hand? Nature

produces effortlessly, Aristotle feels, without calculations and with a perfection in execution that far surpasses human artisanal making. It is in any case Aristotle's view that the world could not have been 'made', since it can have no beginning, but is eternal. Plotinus and his school would have been reminded of these views by the commentaries of Alexander of Aphrodisias, where it is stressed that nature does not need to calculate in its productions and that human craft is a poor imitation of nature.

Other philosophical schools also rejected Plato's cosmic demiurge. For the Stoics the divine productive force works from *within* matter and not upon matter. The Epicureans ridiculed the idea of a toiling god working (with what tools?) to produce the world. They felt in any case—but this was a minority view—that the world is not well made and that it is impious to impute a botched job to the gods. The world results rather from the irrational, arbitrary movements of atoms in the void.

Given such criticisms, what was a Platonist to make of the demiurge of the *Timaeus*? Many Platonists reacted by claiming that Plato's story was not to be taken literally. They shared Aristotle's view that the world was eternal and therefore that strictly speaking it was not 'made'. Others disagreed, for example Atticus (fragment 4), insisting that the *Timaeus* ascribed a beginning to the world. Those who claimed that the world was eternal and not 'made' at a particular moment had to interpret Plato's divine demiurge accordingly. One such interpretation can be found in Alcinous, *Didaskalikos*, chapter 14: when Plato says

that the world is generated, we must take this to mean not that there was a time when the world did not exist, but that the world is always becoming and reveals a more fundamental cause of its existence. And the soul of the world, existing always, is not made by God, but ordered by him. *And God is said to make in this sense*, that he awakens and turns the mind of the world-soul to him . . . so that it [soul] will contemplate his thoughts [i.e. the Forms] and receive the Forms.

The world, according to Alcinous, results from the combination of independent causes, a transcendent god, a world-soul, and matter. God does not produce soul and matter, but merely inspires soul to organize matter after the model provided by his thoughts, the Forms. The purpose of all this is both to show how the world is eternally made and to allow god to function as a cause without involving him in any demeaning artisanal action: he lives, as undisturbed as Aristotle's divine intellect, in the perfection of his thought. His cosmic tasks are performed by a subordinate, world-soul.

How satisfactory is this? As a reading of Plato's text it seems no more far-fetched than some other interpretations. But as a theory it hardly solves the problems posed by Plato's assimilation of natural to artisanal production. It merely delegates god's artisanal tasks to a subordinate. How then does soul 'make' the world? Does it work like a craftsman? If not, how does it operate? To these questions we might add a difficulty that is relevant in particular to Plotinus. Alcinous' account and in general the image of artisanal production assume that the world is constituted from the co-operation of a variety of pre-existing independent causes. However, for Plotinus there cannot be this combination of independent causes: the world must derive from one ultimate source, the One, through the intermediary stages of intellect and soul. Thus for him soul, and only soul, is the proximate cause of the world.

2. Production as Contemplation (*Ennead* III. 8 [30]. 1–7)

In the first works he wrote Plotinus shows awareness of the difficulties involved in comparing the genesis of the world with the artisanal production of an object. He accepts the Aristotelian claim that natural processes are far superior to human craft: nature does not need to calculate and deliberate; it does not toil over its work (see IV. 8 [6]. 8. 14–16). How then is the world produced? How is Plato's *Timaeus* to be read?

One approach to an answer can be found in IV. 8 [6]. 2. 19–30:

This is why our soul, he [Plato] says, were it to be with the perfect soul, would, having been perfected, 'travel above and direct the whole universe' [*Phaedrus*, 246c]; when it ceases from being in bodies or belonging to a body, then, like world-soul, it will join in governing without difficulty the universe. . . . For the care of the universe is double, a general ordering by the uninvolved command of royal rulership, and a care of the particular through applied action by means of contact of the maker with what is made.

This text seems to push even further the solution found in Alcinous, which consists in saving higher causes from involvement in the actual work of making by assigning this work to subordinates, rather as a ruler—the image is now political—might delegate menial tasks to his minions. (The delegation of tasks to subordinates appears already in the *Timaeus* (41ac), where the demiurge hands over lesser work to lower gods.) In Alcinous the work is transferred from god to world-soul; in Plotinus it is transferred from this soul to particular souls. As in the case of Alcinous, this approach will not do: merely transferring artisanal tasks does not eliminate and replace them, which is what is required if one accepts, as Plotinus does, the criticisms of artisanal making as a way of understanding the genesis of things.

We can find in Plotinus' later writings the elements of an account of the constitution of the world that does not invoke the process of artisanal production with all its attendant defects (calculation, worry, uncertainty, toil). The fullest text is III. 8 [30]. 1–7, which is the opening of the large anti-Gnostic treatise (III. 8, V. 8, V. 5, II. 9). Although one can easily read the text simply as Plotinus' response to difficulties traditionally associated with Plato's *Timaeus*, it becomes clear later in the treatise that these difficulties were made more acute by the influence in Plotinus' school of the Gnostic notion that the world was produced by a cosmic demiurge who had, in ignorance, fabricated something evil, this world. Plotinus regarded such notions as a perverse reading of Plato's *Timaeus*: 'And they lie completely about him [Plato] as regards the way in which the world is made and much else, debasing his views as if they had understanding of intelligible nature' (II. 9. 6. 24–7). Plotinus had referred, earlier in the treatise, to the ignorance of the Gnostics as to how the world is produced:

Therefore they are wrong to destroy and generate [the world] in this way, while the intelligible remains, as if the maker at one point wished to make.

They do not wish to understand how the world is made, nor do they know that in so far as the intelligible illuminates, the rest never lacks. (V. 8. 12. 20–4)

It is at the beginning of the anti-Gnostic treatise, in III. 8, that a correct understanding of the production of the world is developed.

Plotinus starts out by proposing a thesis which he thinks will be considered strange:

What if at first in play before undertaking to be serious we were to say that everything desires contemplation and looks to this goal, not only rational but also irrational animals and the nature in plants and the earth that generates them, and that all reach it as far as their nature permits . . . could anyone tolerate such a strange claim? (1. 1–8)

That humans seek after contemplation (*theoria*) as the full possession of the highest knowledge may be plausible, at least as a thesis. (Aristotle points to this thesis in the famous opening words of the *Metaphysics*.) But that this knowledge could also be the goal of irrational things seems hardly credible.

In developing his thesis further, Plotinus suggests that the other forms of human activity (distinguished by Aristotle) besides contemplation, that is, acting and making, are subordinate to contemplation: we act and make things for the sake of contemplation, as a kind of by-product resulting from contemplation (as when the geometer produces diagrams as a consequence of his thinking, 4. 9–11), or as a lesser form or substitute for contemplation:

And indeed men, whenever they become too feeble to contemplate, undertake action as a shadow of contemplation and reason. For since the weakness of their souls does not make contemplating fit for them, not being able sufficiently to grasp the object of contemplation, and through this not being fulfilled, yet desiring to see it, they are brought to action, so as to see what they cannot grasp with intellect. Thus whenever they make, they themselves want to see it and they want others to contemplate and perceive whenever their intention as far as possible becomes action. We will find then in all cases that making and action are a weakness or a side-effect of contemplation, a weakness if one has nothing after the action, a side-effect if one has something else that is superior to the action to contemplate. (4. 31–43; see also ch. 6)

Allowing the claim that, when we do or make something, this occurs as a consequence of, or as a substitute for, knowing, we need to see how this claim can be applied beyond the human realm, to all levels of the natural world.

Nature, as the power of soul that organizes matter, does not work on matter, as it were, 'with its hands' or with instruments (ch. 2). Rather it is a form which produces without moving, since in all production, including artisanal making, there is something which does not move or change, the form guiding the process, and since it is in matter that changes occur and that visible shapes are generated in accord with this form. (On this see also above, Ch. 2 s. 6.) As the unmoving rational principle responsible for form in matter it must be contemplation:

> For action happens in accord with a rational principle [*logos*] from which it is different. But the rational principle, even that which accompanies action and directs, is not action. If therefore it is not action, but rational principle, it is contemplation. And in all rational principle the lowest [level] derives from contemplation. (3. 3–7)

In describing nature, the formative principle of things, as contemplation, Plotinus does not wish to suggest that it thinks in the sense that it calculates, enquires, deliberates (3. 14–17). Such thinking would imply deficiency, a lack of some knowledge that must be sought:

> But it [nature] has, and it is through having that it makes. Thus it is in being what it is that it makes, and as much as it is, it makes. But it is contemplation and object of contemplation, because it is a rational principle. Thus it is in being contemplation and object of contemplation and rational principle that it makes in as much as it is these. So making emerges for us as contemplation. For it is the product of a contemplation that remains and does nothing else, but makes in being contemplation. (3. 16–23)

Thus nature does not try to figure out how it should design the world. Rather, the world reflects a certain knowledge in nature, a contemplation inspired by higher principles. Thus, as Plotinus says later in the anti-Gnostic treatise,

> you can say for what reason the earth is in the middle, why it is round, and why the ecliptic is as it is. But there [in the intelligible] it is not the case that

all was planned thus because it had to be in this way, but rather it is because [the intelligible] is as it is that [the world] is very well arranged. (V. 8. 7. 36–40)

Why things are made in the way they are resolves into the fact that things are made in accord with the nature of their maker: nature as contemplating soul which contemplates intellect.

Summing up we can say then (1) that natural production does not involve toiling: nature as the form guiding changes in matter does not itself change; and (2) that it does not involve calculations: nature as a form of knowledge complete in itself is simply reflected as such in the 'design' of the world. In both respects nature's productivity is not artisanal.

Plotinus is aware of course that speaking of nature as a form of contemplation or knowledge means stretching these terms beyond their normal (human) application. Nature as contemplation is neither perception nor understanding. Rather, it is a very low form of consciousness comparable to the consciousness of one who is asleep (III. 8. 4. 22–4). It is the lowest form of consciousness in a series of levels of contemplation going up through soul to intellect (4. 8–13). As intellect exists as a contemplation of the One, and as soul exists as a contemplation of intellect, so is nature a contemplation of soul whose consequence, a kind of by-product, is the world (cf. chs. 5–8). Thus, in III. 8, Plotinus definitively replaces the artisanal mode of world-making with a process of contemplative derivation: the world derives from soul in the same way that soul derives from intellect and intellect from the One.

3. Nature, Time, and Matter

The account of the generation of the world in III. 8 requires development in a number of respects. (1) We might wish to know more, for example, about this contemplative 'nature' of which Plotinus speaks in III. 8 and its relationship to soul. (2) What of the question of the eternity of the world and how does time emerge? (3) And what of the ultimate matter in which bodies are constituted? Is it also produced by nature?

1. Nature, as a productive force, is perhaps best regarded as that aspect of the power of soul whose activity corresponds to the basic organization of the world. Soul includes a range of powers or activities which manifest themselves in the various living functions characterizing soul's presence in body (see above, Ch. 1 s. 3); nature is part of this range of powers. In this sense nature is not a reality separate from soul in the same way that soul is a reality separate from intellect. In some texts Plotinus speaks of nature as an image produced by soul (see V. 2 [11]. 1. 18–21) and this is the impression given in III. 8. 1–5. Yet Plotinus also distinguishes between soul and its lower powers, on the one hand, and intellect and soul, on the other, by speaking of soul as moving in producing these lower functions and of intellect as immobile in its production of soul. This dynamism peculiar to soul expresses the continuity of nature linking soul and its lower functions (see V. 2. 1. 22–9, III. 4 [15]. 1. 1–6, III. 8. 5). If nature is, as a productive force, an integral part of soul, the *effect* soul has on matter, the life it lends to matter and which constitutes with matter a living body, can be described as an image or 'trace' or 'shadow' of soul (see VI. 4 [22]. 15. 15–18, IV. 4 [28]. 18. 1–9).

2. If Plotinus does not interpret the *Timaeus* literally as regards the image of the divine craftsman, he also does not understand the text as assigning a beginning moment to the world. Like other Platonists such as Alcinous, he accepts the Aristotelian doctrine that the world has no beginning and interprets the *Timaeus* as illustrating the eternal constitution of the world by transcendent causes. The world derives eternally from soul just as soul and intellect derive eternally from the One. In producing the world, soul acts in such a way that time emerges as characteristic of the world. Time, Plotinus concludes in a fine and well-argued analysis of the subject in III. 7 [45], is produced by soul which, not content to remain in contemplation of intellect, expresses this contemplation in a movement that is a fragmentation and spreading out into a succession of the unified life of intellect (ch. 11). This breaking up of unified life into successive moments is time: 'time is the life of soul in the movement of passage from one mode of life to another' (11. 43–5). In being made by, and in, the movement of soul that is time,

the world is time-bound. It lives in successive fragments the unity of life in intellect which is eternity.

3. It has been felt by some modern readers of Plotinus that the matter in which soul generates the world is independent of soul, pre-existing soul's making of the world in much the same way that it does in Alcinous. If this were indeed the case, Plotinus would not be consistent in applying the Principle of Prior Simplicity according to which everything must derive, directly or indirectly, from the One. If the world is produced according to the system of derivation that Plotinus worked out for the higher levels of reality (the derivation of intellect and of soul), then one would expect matter to emerge as a sort of secondary activity of nature which is undefined and which, through 'turning' in some way toward nature as the lowest level of soul, is formed by the model that nature represents. Plotinus did indeed think along these lines, as we can see in III. 4 [15]:

Just as everything generated prior to this was generated shapeless and was formed by turning towards the generator and was nourished, as it were, thus indeed was this, when generated, no longer a form of soul, being lifeless, but complete indetermination. For if indetermination is found at higher levels, it is indeterminate in form, not being something completely indeterminate, but [indeterminate] in relation to its perfection. But this is now total indetermination. When completed it becomes body, taking a shape suitable to its capacity. (III. 4 [15]. 1. 8–15)

Matter is not then an independent cause; it ultimately derives, as does everything else, from the One. As absolute indeterminateness it is the end of the process of derivation. In it appear lifeless images of soul which as such can carry no further the expression of the power and perfection of the One.

8

Evil

1. The Problem of Evil

The Principle of Prior Simplicity (above, Ch. 4) requires that everything derive, directly or indirectly, from the One. Thus the material world derives indirectly, through soul, from the One: soul produces matter in which, in relation to soul, the world is constituted. But the material world is by no means perfect. Plotinus does not attempt to minimize the presence in it of various sorts of evil. Is he saying, therefore, that soul, by nature an expression of the good, produces evil? Since he describes matter as absolute evil (below, s. 2), is he not claiming that ultimately the absolute good (the One) produces absolute evil (matter)? Is this not self-contradictory? It is Plotinus' belief (above, Ch. 6 s. 2) that what is good expresses its perfection, giving of its goodness. How then could it produce evil?

Such questions inevitably arise in connection with philosophies which propose one ultimate source of reality and identify this source as good. Such philosophies seem obliged to choose between denying the reality of evil; trying to live with the apparent contradiction in saying that the good produces evil; or giving up the claim that there is only one ultimate source of things (a position to which we can refer as 'monism'), admitting two opposing sources, a principle of good and a principle of evil (a position we will call 'dualism'). Such problems occur also of course in religious thought when god is taken to be both good and the unique creator of things. They had become part of the Greek philosophical tradition long before Plotinus faced them.

Plotinus quotes texts from Plato's *Theaetetus* (176a) which say that evil is a permanent feature of this world: ' "Evils will not be destroyed", but are "necessary", and are not to be found "among the gods", but "wander about mortal nature and this place forever" ' (I. 8 [51]. 6. 1–4). Plotinus recalls also (I. 8. 7. 1–7) that Plato, in the *Timaeus* (47e–48a), describes the world as resulting from two opposing principles, intellect, which is good but which does not completely prevail over the opposing principle, 'necessity'. To what is defective and evil in the universe we ought to add moral evil or vice among humans. Several passages concerning this in Plato's *Phaedo* and *Phaedrus* are discussed by Plotinus in IV. 8 [6]. Why do souls sin? Why do they fall? Why are they imprisoned in the body and punished? And what is the relation between this moral evil and the evil that is a permanent feature of the universe?

Evil is more prominent in Plato's universe than in Aristotle's, where reigns a rational order in which each thing usually realizes its appropriate perfection. The order is fairly loose: things sometimes (but not normally) go wrong; some malfunction, obstacle, or chance event might produce failures in natural processes and in the human moral sphere. Such looseness was not tolerated in the Stoic universe, since it was permeated and controlled by an immanent rational god. This meant that everything had to be, in one way or another, good. Such a radical thesis makes evil, of course, a particularly acute problem, a problem which could threaten the very coherence of Stoicism. In replying to their critics, the Stoics tried to argue that evil is a feature of a whole which is good: what we consider as evils (catastrophes, injustices, etc.) have in fact a role to play in a larger plan which is good. If only we could see the 'whole picture' we could understand, for example, how suffering serves a good purpose. And since the world is a complex system it must be varied and include features which we, judging things in isolation, consider bad but which form a necessary part of the goodness of the whole.

As background to Plotinus' discussion of the problem of evil, we should also take into account the ways in which Middle Platonists interpreted Plato. In general their approach was dualistic: the world is constituted from two opposite principles, good (the demiurge and the Forms) and evil (matter and/or a soul as the cause of disorderly motion in matter). If more convenient for explaining evil, this dualism was not an option open to the monist Plotinus. He was finally confronted with the Gnostic notion of evil as the apostasy of a demiurge who made this world, an evil work, as a result of an act of self-assertion and revolt from the good.

2. Matter as Absolute Evil (*Ennead* I. 8 [51])

In the first chapters of I. 8 Plotinus tries to say what the nature of evil actually is. To do this he takes its opposite, the nature of the good. The good has to do with self-sufficiency, measure, form, perfection, either as their source (the One) or as they characterize intellect and soul. It is thus what is 'beyond being' or is 'being' in the sense that it is the complete and perfect kind of being possessed by intelligible reality (ch. 2). Evil, as the opposite of the good, can then be described by opposition as non-being, not in the sense that it does not exist, but in the sense that it is the opposite of the perfect type of existence found in soul, intellect, and the One. It is thus the opposite of self-sufficiency, measure, form, perfection:

For one might already reach a notion of this [evil] as a lack of measure in relation to measure, and lack of limit in relation to limit, and formlessness in relation to what is formative, and permanent deficiency in relation to what is self-sufficient, always indeterminate, in no way stable, affected in every way, unfulfilled, total poverty. (3. 12–16)

There is in Plotinus' world a reality which corresponds to this description, a reality which of its very nature is absolute absence of form and measure: matter. The descriptions of evil and matter are identical. Matter is evil (3. 35–40).

We can refer to matter as 'absolute' or primary evil, or evil *per se*, as a way of distinguishing between it and things which come to share in evil through some kind of association with matter, although they are not evil in themselves. Such 'secondary' evils include bodies, which are constituted in matter (4. 1–5), and souls, which become evil by association with lack of measure (4. 6–13). Disease, for example, is a lack of measure in a body and ugliness a lack of form (5. 22–4):

Let then primary evil be that which is without measure, whereas that which finds itself in the unmeasured by assimilation or participation is by virtue of an accidental property secondary evil. And the darkness is primary and what is darkened secondary in this way. Now vice, being ignorance and lack of measure in the soul, is secondary evil and not evil itself. Nor is virtue the primary good, but it is what is assimilated to or participates in it. (8. 37–45)

Before going further it might be useful to emphasize two points. (1) Body is not in itself evil; it is evil only to the extent that the matter in it does not lend itself to form. (2) The notion of evil as defined by Plotinus as the 'privation' or absence of good is found in Christian thinkers influenced by Plotinus such as Gregory of Nyssa or Augustine. But by 'privation of the good' the Christian theologians mean, not an existing reality, but a wilful turning away of the soul from god. However, evil exists for Plotinus, it is matter, even though he also finds, as we shall see, a turning away of soul from the good. As an existing reality which is part of the universe and is the principle of other evils (including moral evil), we might call matter 'metaphysical evil'.

If evil exists as a reality, how can Plotinus deal with the difficulties sketched at the beginning of this chapter? How can absolute good produce absolute evil? One possible answer (see III. 2 [47]. 5. 27–32) might consist in pointing out that the theory of derivation implies that each successive stage in derivation represents a lesser degree of perfection or (expressing this negatively) a greater degree of imperfection. The series of stages must continue until it reaches its limit, absolute imperfection or evil. It would seem then that it is in the very logic of derivation and of the productivity of the good that evil ultimately be generated.

This answer needs modification. It suggests that derivation means degrees of intensification of imperfection leading to absolute imperfection, which means degrees of intensification of evil leading to absolute evil. But Plotinus does not admit the presence of any form of evil on the two levels of reality below the One:

And [intellect] is the first activity of it [the One] and the first being, while [the One] stays in itself. But it is an activity around it [the One] as if living around it. And soul, dancing outside around it [intellect], looks to it and contemplating what is within sees the god through it. And this is the carefree and blessed 'life of the gods' [*Phaedrus*, 248a]. And there is no evil there, and had all stayed there, there would be no evil, but a first and then second and third goods. (I. 8. 2. 21–8)

We must distinguish then between the existence of degrees of perfection (relative to the One) and the existence of various forms of evil. Things on a lower level than the One, for example soul, can be perfect at their level (cf. 5. 6–8). The derivation of lower levels from the Good does not seem to necessitate the existence of evil (see also II. 9 [33]. 13. 28–34). And yet it does seem that evil is required by derivation in the sense that derivation must come to an end, beyond which the good does not continue to produce:

It is also possible to grasp the necessity of evil in this way. For since there is not only the Good, there must be, in the going out beyond it, or, if one wishes to say it in this way, in the descent and departure, the end beyond which nothing more emerges, and this is evil. There must be something after the first and so also the last, but this is matter, having nothing of the first. (I. 8. 7. 16–23)

It remains the case, however, that matter, as absolute evil, is not just the end of derivation. It is also the *result* of derivation: matter is produced by soul. We are left with the unresolved paradox that the good, which in Plotinus' view ought to give of itself, of its goodness, in fact produces evil.

3. Moral Evil (*Enneads* III. 9 [13]. 3, IV. 8 [6])

In some texts, written earlier in his literary career, Plotinus appears to be suggesting that evil originates in the soul as a consequence of an act of self-assertion which cuts it off from intelligible reality:

but when [soul] is brought to what is lower than it, this is non-being. Soul makes this whenever it turns to itself. Wishing to be in relation to itself, it makes what comes after, an image of itself, non-being, stepping in the void, as it were, and becoming more indeterminate. And the image of this, the indeterminate, is completely dark, for it is irrational and unintelligible as a whole and at a far distance from being. Being in the middle, [soul] is in its place, but looking again as if with a second glance, it shaped the image and in delight goes to it. (III. 9 [13]. 3. 8–16)

And in V. 1 [10]. 1. 1–6 Plotinus says that the 'cause of evil' for souls is an act of self-affirmation which cuts them off from the above.

Such passages give the impression that Plotinus is thinking along lines that recall Gnosticism: evil originates in an apostasy of soul from the Good, an apostasy in which soul makes and forms matter. Thus metaphysical evil, we might conclude, is not a product of the Good, the result of derivation. It is created by *moral* evil, a moral failure in soul.

This conclusion is not compatible with Plotinus' position, later in *Ennead* I. 8, that moral evil is secondary and dependent on metaphysical evil, which is primary. Nor does it fit with what is said in another early writing, IV. 8 [6]. In this treatise Plotinus discusses the reasons for soul's descent to the body. He points out that Plato does not speak clearly about this (1. 23–8). In some dialogues (*Phaedo*, *Phaedrus*) Plato regards the association of soul with body as bad, saying that soul is imprisoned in the body, whereas elsewhere (*Timaeus*) soul's presence in the body is seen in a positive way: soul came to body in order to perfect it. In what follows Plotinus emphasizes the point of view of the *Timaeus* as primary: soul is in body as an expression of goodness, as perfecting body.

Thus, although [soul] is divine and from a higher realm, it enters into body and being the lowest divinity comes down in this way through a self-willed inclination and because of its power and direction of what comes after it. If it escapes quickly, it suffers no harm in acquiring knowledge of evil and knowing the nature of vice, showing forth its powers, its works, and creations which, had they remained in the incorporeal, would have been in vain in not proceeding into activity. And soul itself would not notice what it had, since this did not emerge and progress outwards. (5. 24–33)

Soul in making things does not act out of moral evil and such evil does not necessarily appear in its activity. It is prolonged association with the body, a preoccupation and fascination with it, that leads soul to forget itself and become evil (4. 13–30). Metaphysical evil is not produced by a moral failure in soul. Soul's productivity is essentially good. Moral evil arises through the ignorance brought about by infatuation with body. Thus body (and therefore matter) must exist already for moral evil to occur. Moral evil is a consequence, and not a cause, of metaphysical evil. Plotinus' views on this had not changed when he wrote, much later, *Ennead* I. 8 (see the passage quoted immediately below).

But how could metaphysical evil produce moral evil? This would mean that matter prevails over soul, the inferior over the superior, which seems impossible. Is there some flaw in soul that allows it to be influenced by matter? Plotinus insists that this is not the case:

The fall of soul is this, going to matter in this way and weakening because all [its] powers are not present in order to act since matter prevents this presence by holding the place which soul has and making it contract, so to speak, making evil what it takes as if by theft, until soul is able to ascend. So matter is the cause of weakness in the soul and of vice. [Matter] is thus prior evil and primary evil. (I. 8. 14. 44–51)

Yet it is hard to see how matter could be entirely responsible for soul's vice. This would mean robbing soul of moral responsibility for its actions. In a treatise written not long before, III. 2 [47], Plotinus argues for a measure of moral responsibility in soul in the framework of a world organized by intelligible principles: we do not do evil because this is so determined by the order of things.

Living beings which have a self-willed movement incline sometimes to the better things, sometimes to the worse. It is perhaps not worth enquiring about the turning of oneself to the worse. For at first what is a slight turn, in progressing, always makes the error far greater. And body accompanies and necessarily desire. And if attention is not paid to the first step and what happens suddenly and if it is not rectified at once, a commitment is generated to that to which one fell. (III. 2. 4. 36–44; see III. 3. 4. 47–8)

It seems that it takes a minimal wayward movement in soul, a minor impulse, for it to slip gradually into subjection to the body. This fall means a turning away from intellect, therefore ignorance and the emergence of moral evil.

4. The Goodness of the Universe (*Ennead* III. 2–3 [47–8])

Why do we do evil? Is it through the force of the circumstances in which we live? Is it because of some flaw in our nature? Or because of some perverse choice? Why this choice? Plotinus goes very far in insisting on the natural goodness of soul and on the importance of metaphysical evil (matter and secondarily bodies as formed in matter) as the occasion of moral evil. But he cannot make metaphysical evil the only factor producing moral evil, for this would destroy our control over our lives and our moral responsibility. Some movement on our part as souls must initiate our growth into vice. But Plotinus seeks to minimize this movement and it remains something of a mystery.[1]

If metaphysical evil does not by itself produce moral evil, neither does moral evil produce metaphysical evil: soul does not (as in certain kinds of Gnosticism) produce matter and bodies on account of some moral failure. But this brings us back again to the paradox that the Good makes evil. The productivity of the Good entails derivation and therefore lower degrees of perfection, but this does not seem to necessitate at first the presence of evil. Evil appears later, at the end or limit of derivation. But why must this end to derivation occur at the stage just after soul?. Why does soul, which is good, make matter, which is evil?

The dilemmas involved in Plotinus' theory of evil are not easily resolved. If we wish to analyse them further we should examine also the discussion of evil in III. 2–3 [47–8]. Plotinus attempts to defend here the notion of 'providence' (which he interprets as the order given to this world by intellect) against the Epicureans who deny its existence, pointing to the defects of the world, and against Gnostics who saw the world as the work of an evil demiurge (III. 2. 1. 5–10). Plotinus surveys the inventory of evils that beset us—perhaps the difficult political and economic conditions prevailing at the time (see above, Introduction s. 1) made them all too vivid. On the whole he adopts the optimism of the Stoics, making use of their arguments, with suitable Platonic adjustments: many of the reverses we suffer

---

[1] Plotinus also tries to minimize soul's implication in evil by confining it to the lower aspects of soul (I. 8. 4. 25–33).

(e.g. poverty) are not really evils; many evils serve a good purpose; the wicked will ultimately be punished; although the wicked are responsible for their acts, these acts are integrated into a larger cosmic scheme which is good; the goodness and beauty of this scheme require diversity, differences in perfection, just as a good play must include villains as well as heroes. Not all of these arguments—many are traditional—are convincing. We need to believe in the transmigration of the soul if we are to accept that

It is not by coincidence that one is a slave; one does not happen to be a prisoner of war; one is not randomly violated in one's body. But there was a time when one did what one now suffers. And he who kills his mother will be [reborn] a woman to be killed by her child. And the rapist will be [reborn] a woman to be raped. (III. 2. 13. 11–15)

Be that as it may (it was probably far more convincing to Plotinus' contemporaries than it would be to us), it is clear from the argument of III. 2–3 that for Plotinus this world is, despite the presence of various evils, a place illuminated everywhere by beauty, goodness, and intelligence. The same very positive attitude to the world is found a little later in the last words of the treatise where Plotinus explores the idea of matter as absolute evil:

But evil is not just evil, due to the power and nature of good. Since if it has appeared of necessity, it is enclosed in beautiful bonds, like certain prisoners bound with gold, and is concealed by these, so as not to be seen by the gods and so that men need not always see evil, but when they look they are accompanied by images of beauty as reminders. (I. 8. 15. 23–9)

9

Beauty

1. The Experience of Beauty (*Ennead* I. 6 [1])

An aspect of life of great interest to Plato is the experience of beauty. He includes in this experience not only perceptual beauty (the beauty of nature and art that we see and hear), but also non-perceptual or immaterial beauty such as that of the virtues of soul and of intellect (*Hippias major*, 297e–298b; *Symposium*, 210ac). This range in the kinds of beauty, as Plato sees it, is sketched by Plotinus as follows: 'The beautiful occurs mostly in sight, but it is found also in hearing, in groups of words, and it is in all [kinds of] music. . . . But there are also, for those who progress upwards from sense-perception, beautiful pursuits and actions and states of character and sciences and the beauty of the virtues' (I. 6 [1]. 1. 1–6). Postponing for the moment discussion of the notion of immaterial beauty, we might first ask how the experience of perceptual beauty is to be explained. Is there some quality or property possessed by some things which makes them (and not others) beautiful? But some of us find something beautiful which others do not. Is it a question of individual taste, of cultural preferences? Beauty then would not actually exist in things as a particular property: it would be 'in the eye of the beholder'. This cliché can do little justice to the experience of beauty as it is described by Plato, an experience whose power, the power of love, seizes us, throws us into confusion, and transforms our lives.

Plato treats of beauty both as a property existing in things which makes them beautiful and as a complex psychological reaction reflecting aspects of the soul of those who experience beauty. It is a property of things in the sense that they are beautiful because they participate in a Form, the Form of beauty, just as things are large by participating in the Form of largeness (*Phaedo*, 100bd). Beauty is therefore a Form, distinct from other Forms, in which some things participate and therefore become beautiful. Plato also analyses the reaction of the soul to the presence of beauty, in particular the reaction of the lover to the beauty of his love (*Phaedrus*, 249d–252a; see *Symposium*, 210a–211c). He sees this reaction as a recollection of the Form of beauty seen by the soul of the lover in a previous existence. Through their participation in the Form of beauty, beautiful objects remind us of our former blissful vision of the higher world of Forms. In some famous pages of the *Phaedrus* (251a–256e) Plato shows how the recognition, remembrance, and desire of a higher existence underlie the aesthetic experience whose intensity is increased by the confusion and pain of the soul seeking to possess a beloved who is a mere image of the beauty that is sought.

Few can reach the artistic, emotional, and spiritual depth of Plato in interpreting the experience of beauty. A more prosaic approach, which dominated in antiquity, was popularized by the Stoics. Plotinus summarizes it thus: 'Everyone, one might say, asserts that it is good proportion of the parts in relation to each other and to the whole, with the addition of the factor of good colour, which makes visual beauty, and to be beautiful for these [visual objects] and for all others is to be proportioned and measured' (I. 6. 1. 20–5). Why add good colour to good proportion in the definition of beauty? Perhaps because good colour was felt in antiquity to be intrinsically beautiful. Plotinus himself believed that good proportion did not necessarily suffice to make a face, for example, beautiful (I. 6. 1. 37–41). But he did not think that adding good colour would be enough (see VI. 7. 22. 27–9).

In his very first composition, I. 6 [1], which would also become in antiquity and in the Renaissance his best-known and most influential work, Plotinus criticizes the Stoic theory of beauty and develops an approach to the subject which owes much to Plato and which also breaks new ground. Plotinus first formulates the question of beauty as follows:

What then is it that is responsible for making bodies appear beautiful and for making sounds attractive, as beautiful, to our hearing? All that which in turn pertains to the soul, how is it beautiful? And are they all [beautiful] by one and the same beauty, or is beauty in body other than beauty in other things? And what might they, or it, be? (1. 7–13)

In the remainder of the first chapter (1) Plotinus presents criticisms of the Stoic theory of beauty. He then develops (2) his own account of perceptual beauty in chapters 2–3. (3) In chapters 4–6 beauty of the soul is examined, which produces the conclusion that that which was identified (in chs. 2–3) as making bodies beautiful is the same as that which makes soul beautiful. This leads (4) to a discussion in the final chapters of the One as the ultimate goal of the lover of beauty.

1. Plotinus argues against the Stoics that if a whole is beautiful because well proportioned, then the elements making up the whole are not beautiful by themselves, but merely contribute to the beauty of the whole. But surely the parts must also be beautiful? How could they be ugly? (1. 26–31) This argument is not convincing. Plotinus himself makes use elsewhere of the Stoic idea that a good painter does not use exclusively beautiful colours, that a good play includes inferior types as well as heroes (III. 2. 11). The Stoics could then easily concede that some parts of a beautiful whole might not themselves be beautiful. A reply to Plotinus might consist in saying that since it is the *proportion* of the parts that determines the beauty of the whole, the parts themselves are, in relation to this beauty, neither beautiful nor ugly. Plotinus also claims that Stoic theory does not allow for beauty in simple (non-composite) objects such as individual colours, light, gold, lightening, individual sounds (1. 32–8; see Plato, *Philebus*, 51cd). One might reply to this by arguing that such simple objects are in fact composite, but it is also true that we see (or hear) them as simple; their beauty *for us* is not that expressed by a proportion. Plotinus goes on (1. 41–53) to attack the plausibility of construing beauty in the soul (virtue, knowledge) as a matter of proportion: what sort of proportion could it be? Inner harmony or consistency? But one can be consistent in vice and in error!

2. Plotinus' criticism of Stoic theory does not go very far. In fact he is willing, as we shall see, to find some truth in this theory. He

prefers however to take another starting-point, our actual experience of beauty: 'Something becomes perceptible even at first sight and soul speaks as if understanding and receives it with recognition and adjusts to it as it were. But looking at the ugly it recoils and refuses it and turns away from it' (2. 2–7). These reactions recall the activity of soul in judging things in relation to the innate concepts possessed by soul as image of intellect (see V. 3. 2. 11–16; 4. 13–19; above, Ch. 3 s. 4). Hence the aesthetic judgement is described as follows: 'The power [of the soul] ordered to it knows it, a power which is most competent for judging what pertains to it . . . or perhaps [the rest of the soul] speaks, adjusting to the Form in it [the soul], and using it [the Form] in its judgement, as a ruler [is used for judging] straightness' (3. 1–5). Plotinus seems then to adhere fairly closely to the Platonic idea that soul recognizes the Form of beauty in bodies which participate in it.

Plotinus sees soul, however, as recalling, not just one Form, but the whole world of Forms: '[Soul] being in its nature what it is, related to the higher kind of being in reality, whatever it sees that is related to it, or a trace of this relation, delights it; it is startled and relates it back to itself and recalls itself and what belongs to it' (2. 7–11). This recollection of intelligible being in general (rather than of just the Form of beauty) seems to be present also in Plato's *Phaedrus*, but Plotinus draws conclusions from this that are new. If the soul recalls intelligible reality in the experience of beauty, and if this recollection is triggered by a relation between beautiful bodies and intelligible being, then bodies are beautiful to the extent that they participate in intelligible reality, that is in *any* Form, not just in a particular Form such as the Form of beauty. 'We say that it is by participation in Form that these [are beautiful]. For all that is shapeless but capable of receiving shape and form, not sharing in reason and form, is ugly and outside divine reason. And this is altogether ugly' (2. 13–16). Form is what makes bodies beautiful and makes us react to them in the way that we do when we recognize Form in them.

It might be objected at this point that the range of things participating in Form is far wider than the range of beautiful things:

Plotinus fails to account for the specific character of beautiful things as distinguished from other formed bodies. A response to this might be to point to degrees in the participation in Form according to which things are more or less beautiful as participating more or less in Form (see V. 8. 9. 43–7). Plotinus would also reject the implication that beauty is not everywhere. He often stresses the great beauty of the world, in opposition, for example, to Gnostic hate for the world (see V. 8. 8). For us today, for whom nature is being transformed into the expression and victim of our desires, the ubiquity of beauty is perhaps less evident.

Plotinus' approach enables him to account for simple beauties (light, colours): they are matter mastered by Form (I. 6. 3. 17–28). He can also incorporate the truth in the Stoic view that good proportion plays a part in beauty: Form is responsible for good proportion: 'As it approaches, then, Form organizes what is to be one whole out of many parts, bringing it to a single completion and making it one through agreement [of the parts]' (2. 18–20).

3. What of the immaterial beauties of soul? What makes them beautiful? Is it that which makes bodies beautiful? Can non-perceptual things such as virtue, we might ask, be properly said to be beautiful? The range in meaning of the Greek word *kalos* ('beautiful'), which can express moral as well as aesthetic values, certainly suggests a continuity between perceptual beauty and moral and intellectual excellence. Plotinus says that just as we cannot talk of visual beauty if we are blind, so we cannot discuss inner spiritual beauty if we have never received it (4. 4–13). He therefore simply assumes our experience of non-perceptual beauty in I. 6 (in V. 8 he provides, as we shall see below, some arguments in support of the idea of immaterial beauty) and tries to identify what is responsible for this beauty.

The approach is through the opposite, 'ugliness' of the soul (5. 22–5). The ugly soul is full of vice, 'intemperate and unjust, filled with many desires, full of turmoil, [living in] fears through cowardice, in envy through pettiness . . . in love with impure pleasures, living the life of whatever it is affected by through the body and taking ugliness as pleasant' (5. 26–31). What accounts for this ugliness? 'Mixing and blending and inclining towards the body and matter' (5. 48–9). If soul is made ugly by its infatuation with body and matter, then it is made beautiful by purification from them and a return to its original self:

Thus when soul is purified it becomes Form and rational principle and altogether incorporeal and intellective and completely part of the divine, whence is the source of beauty and all things of that kind. So when soul is brought up to intellect, it is more beautiful. But intellect and what goes with it is soul's beauty, its very own and not another's, for then is soul truly and solely itself. (6. 13–18)

Virtue makes soul beautiful as a purification (see Plato, *Phaedo*, 69c) bringing soul back to itself and its origin in intellect and the Forms.

Thus intellect or Form (they are one), which makes bodies beautiful, is also that which constitutes the beauty of soul. Participating in and becoming Form is to become beautiful, which implies that Form not only makes things beautiful but is also itself primarily beautiful. Beauty is Form or true being: 'beautifulness is what is true being' (6. 21). The One is the source of the beauty that is intellect,

Soul is beauty through intellect. And the rest is beautiful when shaped by soul, the [beauty] in actions and in pursuits. And indeed those things such as are called bodies are made by soul and are made beautiful by it, since it is divine and as if a part of beauty, when it touches and orders them, to the extent to which they can participate. (6. 27–33)

4. The identification of beauty with Form and intellect is rapidly made in I. 6 and we must go to V. 8 for a fuller discussion. In I. 6 it leads immediately to questions concerning the ascent of the soul to the One, since the pursuit of beauty has become the pursuit of true being and its source, the One or the Good. The experience of material and immaterial beauty is intensified and superseded by the desire of the Good (ch. 7). The ascent, described in two chapters worthy of Plato (chs. 8–9), is made by a purification of the soul which renders it beautiful:

Come back into yourself and look. If you do not yet see yourself as something beautiful, just as the sculptor, to make a beautiful statue, removes this, polishes that, making this smooth and this pure . . . thus should you remove what is superfluous and straighten what is crooked, purifying what is dark, making it shine. (9. 7–12)

Becoming oneself beautiful enables one to approach the source of all beauty, the One.

In the last lines of I. 6 Plotinus describes the One both as primary beauty and as 'beyond' the primary beauty which is intelligible reality. The latter description is what we would expect to be more correct, given Plotinus' identification of beauty with Form. In what sense can the One be itself beautiful or beauty? This issue will be examined below in connection with some chapters of VI. 7.

2. Intelligible Beauty (*Ennead* V. 8 [31])

At the end of V. 8 [31] Plotinus asks: 'Does what has been said suffice in order to lead to a clear understanding of "the intelligible realm" [Plato, *Republic*, 517b], or is it necessary to approach this again, using another path, in this way?' (13. 22–4). The treatise deals therefore with intelligible beauty as a way of increasing understanding of intelligible reality. The same purpose is pursued in the next part of the anti-Gnostic work to which V. 8 belongs, V. 5 [32], where intelligible being is considered from the aspect of the unity of intellect and its object (above, Ch. 3 s. 3), as it had been before at the beginning of the work, III. 8 [30], where the world is shown to derive from intellect as contemplation (above Ch. 7 s. 2). These various approaches to intelligible reality thus act as correctives to a fundamental Gnostic error, as Plotinus sees it: ignorance of the true nature of intelligible being (see above, Ch. 7 s. 2).

V. 8 begins with the following suggestion: 'Let us try to see and to say to ourselves, in as much as these things can be said, how one might contemplate the beauty of intellect and its world' (1. 4–6). To do this Plotinus first argues (chs. 1–2) that the beauty of natural and man-made things derives from form which is itself more beautiful than they. Since it is soul (both cosmic and individual) which produces these things, he then examines (ch. 3) the beauty of form in soul and points to its origin in the higher and more beautiful Forms that are intellect. To approach the beauty of (and that is) intellect, Plotinus explores several paths in the following chapters which serve to lead soul to pure intellection and hence to intellect.

If form makes perceptual objects beautiful (what is said on this here in V. 8. 1–2 could be added to what we can find in I. 6), why should form itself be more beautiful than these objects? Might not beauty be the *perceptible* expression of form which is therefore in itself not beautiful? Plotinus has various reasons for saying that form is more beautiful than the objects which participate in it. The materiality of the perceptible object is indifferent and in fact an impediment (rather than a contribution) to the beauty of the object, in so far as it limits the reception of form: 'For [the beauty] in the skill [of the artist] did not go to the stone, but stayed, and another [beauty was produced] from it, inferior to it. Nor did this [lower beauty] remain pure in itself, nor as it wished, but [came to be] in so far as the stone yielded to skill' (1. 19–22). Plotinus suggests that the artist has access to intelligible being and that his works are materialized (and therefore diminished) expressions of the beauty that is intellect:

But if someone denies value to the arts, because they make by imitating nature, one should say first that natural beings imitate other things. One should also know that they do not simply imitate the visible, but go beyond, to the principles which produce nature. Then they make much from themselves and add what is lacking, for they are in possession of beauty, since Pheidias did not make his [statue of] Zeus according to a perceptible [model], but conceived of Zeus such as he would be, were he to wish to appear before our eyes. (1. 32–41)

This passage is of great interest for the philosophical interpretation and evaluation of art. Plato was notorious for condemning artists as makers of images of images (sense-objects) of Forms (*Republic*, 597b–598c). By seeing the artist as having direct access to intelligible reality and as creative in his works, Plotinus gave art a high value and anticipated the exalted status artists would acquire much later in the Italian Renaissance. However, Plotinus' main interest here is making the point that the beauty produced by art in material objects is diminished, weakened by its materialization: 'All that is distended departs from itself, if it is strength, from strength, if it is heat, from heat, if in general it is power, from power, if beauty, from beauty. And the first maker must in every case be of itself superior to what is made' (1. 27–31). It follows that if material beauty is produced by form, and materialization means weakening of beauty, then form in itself is more beautiful than the perceptual beauty that it produces (see also ch. 2).

If the form in the soul which makes both natural and artistic beauty is more beautiful than its products, it derives from intellect which, for reasons similar to those just given, must be yet more beautiful and in fact primary beauty. How is one to conceive of the immaterial beauty of intellect? Plotinus proposes taking our soul's intellect or rather that of the divine and purifying our notion of it in order to reach some conception of what pure intellect is like: 'as if one takes something in gold as an illustration of all gold, and if this thing is not pure, purifying it, showing by deed or word that it is not all gold, but only this part' (3. 13–16). A series of reflections on divine intellection follows (chs. 4–8). A conception of perfect intellection emerges which is already largely familiar (see above, Ch. 3 s. 3): it is unchanging knowledge, truth identical with being, translucent self-knowledge, mutual omnipresence. Some aspects of divine intellect are stressed: it is not a discursive intellection which moves from premises to conclusions, since it already has and knows its object (chs. 4–6); as the wisdom producing this world, it does not plot or plan its production, but the world arises as an expression of wisdom (ch. 7).

What is the bearing of all this on the question of immaterial beauty? To conceive intellect (or Form) as it is, is to conceive pure beauty. The beauty of Form is not some property of Form, but is Form itself as the unity of divine intellect and its object. Plotinus stresses the identity of beauty with Form which is also true being:

But the power that is there [in the intelligible] has only its being and only its being beautiful. For where would beauty be if deprived of being? Where would being be if deprived of being beautiful? For in being deprived of beauty, it lacks in being. Therefore being is an object of desire, because the same as beauty, and beauty is object of love, because it is being. What need is there to seek after which is the cause of which, since it is one nature? (9. 36–42)

If there still is difficulty in conceiving of such beauty, it is due, Plotinus would argue, to our not being in a state that makes such an experience possible. We must change from being mere spectators of external material beauty to becoming beautiful in ourselves, to becoming intellect:

But only the exterior impression is recognized by those who do not see the whole, whereas in the case of those who are as it were altogether drunk and filled with nectar [see Plato, *Symposium*, 203b], since beauty goes through all of soul, it is not for them to become mere spectators. For there is no longer in their case something outside, that which sees being also outside, but he who sees sharply has the object of seeing within himself. (10. 32–7)

Or, as Plotinus says a few lines earlier: 'He sees . . . beauty whole, and participates in beauty there [in the intelligible]. For it shines on all and fills those who come there, so they also become beautiful, just as men who climb lofty places are often filled with the golden red colour of the earth there, resembling the earth on which they walk' (10. 23–9). The experience of beauty outside and in another points to and is superseded by the experience of becoming oneself this beauty through a return to one's original self and to intellect, whose beauty one 'sees' as being it, as intellect 'sees' itself. The aesthetic experience becomes the movement in terms of which Plotinus interprets so much else in our lives, the movement of return to our inner self, to self-knowledge: 'Since, whenever we are beautiful, it is by being possessed of ourselves, and we are ugly when we change over to another nature. And knowing ourselves we are beautiful, and ugly when we do not know ourselves' (13. 19–22).

3. Beauty and the One (*Ennead* VI. 7 [38])

In I. 6 Plotinus touches on, but does not discuss in detail, the issue of the relation between beauty and the One. Is the One beautiful or beauty itself? Or is it, as the cause of intellect, 'beyond' or prior to beauty? Since we refer to the One as the Good, what is the relation between beauty and the Good?

Shortly after V. 8, in V. 5 [32]. 12, Plotinus distinguishes sharply between beauty and the Good. Love of beauty is more restricted than love of the Good: desire of the Good is both conscious and unconscious, but love of beauty presupposes awareness of it (12. 9–16); the Good can satisfy all desire whereas beauty does not seem to be an ultimate and universal object of desire (12. 19–25). Beauty can even distract us away from the Good: 'And it [the Good] is mild, well-disposed, more delicate, present to him who wishes, whereas [beauty] involves amazement and shock and pleasure mixed with pain. And indeed it pulls those who do not know away from the Good, as the loved one, being younger, [attracts] away from the father' (12. 33–7). This subordination of beauty to the Good is consistent with Plotinus' argument slightly earlier (in V. 8) that beauty is Form (or intellect) and consequently inferior to the Good, which is the One beyond Form.

However the distinction between beauty and the Good ought not to be pressed to the point of losing sight of the status of intellect as expression of the power of the One. This status is described later, in connection with beauty, in some chapters of VI. 7 [38]. Plotinus says there that it is the presence (the 'light', 'grace', or 'life') of the Good in beauty which moves us and which we desire (22. 11–18). The attractiveness of intelligible beauty derives from the light or 'colour' lent it by the Good. The Good, as beyond Form, is formless, infinite, and the love for it correspondingly infinite (32. 24–8). As the source of intelligible beauty it can be described as 'beauty above beauty. For not being something, what beauty would it be? But being an object of love, it would be what generates beauty. Therefore as the power of all it is the flower of beauty, beauty maker of beauty' (32. 29–32). A little later (33. 20) Plotinus refers to the Good as the 'super-beautiful'. This ought to remind us that the subject of discussion is beyond knowledge and description (see above, Ch. 5). We can speak of the One or the Good as beautiful or as beauty in the sense that it is its presence, its light or 'colour', that generates the beauty of things. It is the light or 'colour' of Form that produces and shines through the beauty of well-proportioned bodies; it is the light of the Good that produces and shines through intelligible beauty. In a manner of speaking then we can say that the source of this light is 'beauty above beauty'.

10

The Return of Soul: Philosophy and Mysticism

1. The Goal of Life

Much of what has been discussed in the preceding chapters is relevant to reaching an understanding of the human condition as Plotinus sees it: deriving from divine intellect, we are souls whose nature it is, as expressions of the One, to organize and perfect material existence. Our love of the One (the Good), from which everything of value comes, may however be overlaid by infatuation with our works, with material things, which causes us to forget ourselves, to become ignorant, evil, and unhappy. Release from vice and misery comes by turning our attention back to the One and reaching it as far as possible. Before looking more closely at the way in which the One can be attained, it may be useful first to place Plotinus' views on human happiness in the broader context of Greek ethical theory.

It has often been remarked that Greek ethical theory is 'eudaimonistic', that is that it deals primarily with that which makes life satisfying, successful, complete, what constitutes *eudaimonia*, a term one might translate with the expression 'well-being' or with the (somewhat anaemic and subjective) word 'happiness'. Given disagreement about what it is that constitutes happiness, what the human good is, ancient philosophers were chiefly concerned with determining the nature of this good. Ethical or moral principles as we think of them now, virtues and vices, were dealt with as a secondary matter since it was assumed that virtue was no more than the appropriate way in which to attain the good for man.

Plato seems at first glance to have diverging conceptions of happiness. On the one hand he follows Socrates in thinking of it as realized in social and political life: it is participating in the life of a city in which all action is based on real knowledge of ethical principles. On the other hand he sometimes suggests, particularly in the *Phaedo*, that happiness lies in escape from the body and blissful vision of the Forms in a higher existence. These two conceptions come together in the Utopia of the *Republic*: the escape from the material world and vision of the Forms are steps taken by the future leaders of the ideal city so that they may on the basis of their knowledge of the Forms (including especially the Form of the Good) govern the life of the city. Happiness is a correct functioning of man and society, of man when his desires and actions are controlled by reason, of society when the needs of citizens are managed by rulers who know and are guided by the Forms.

Aristotle's approach to the question of happiness is similar: happiness is a correct functioning of human nature and of the political structures it produces. Aristotle of course rejects Plato's Forms: there is no question of 'escape' from the body to contemplate the Forms. Virtues and the human good can be known by observing human nature as it functions well. However, in considering intellect to be a divine element in man, Aristotle finds himself saying that the greatest happiness, the highest good for man, is the life of contemplation or knowledge (*theoria*), a life characteristic of the divine (*Nicomachean Ethics*, 10. 7–8). Modern commentators on Aristotle are not agreed as to how his call to man to live the life of the gods is to be reconciled with his view of happiness as the correct functioning of man as a 'political animal' involved in society, having family, friends, and material possessions.

For the Stoics and the Epicureans the good life is also a matter of correct functioning, or functioning in accord with nature. Of course their conceptions of nature diverged. Life according to nature for the Stoics meant obeying the order imposed on the world by the immanent rational god and acting (since we have a share in divine reason) as masters of the judgements and actions that lie in our power. Emerging in a world of unstable conglomerates of atoms, Epicurean man could at most hope to preserve his nature as far as possible, protecting it from disturbance and destruction, living the sober, relatively painless life that he calls pleasure. This life is divine since it approximates for a while to the perfect life enjoyed (between the worlds) by the compounds of fine atoms that are the gods.

When, therefore, Plotinus identifies the human good, the goal of life, as divinization, as 'assimilation to god' (Plato, *Theaetetus*, 176b, quoted by Plotinus in I. 2 [19]. 1. 4 and I. 4 [46]. 16. 10–13), he is making a claim that could be made by many other ancient philosophers. He in turn could have accepted the formulation that the good for man is living in accord with nature. But the way in which he would have understood this formulation would have reflected his new and distinctive views on our nature and its relation to reality, views which might be summarized as follows.

Our nature is not that of some particular entity occupying a fixed place in the structure of reality. As individual souls we are essentially mobile. We can move from life with divine intellect through various kinds of care of the world down to a life of self-degrading enslavement to material things. This wide range in the lives we can lead is possible because, as souls, we are what we do: we can act as beasts and be bestial, we can contemplate like, and thus be, divine intellect (on this see III. 4 [15]). This mobile and Protean self is anchored in the intelligible world. Whatever kind of life we make for ourselves, we remain linked to the above:

And if it is necessary, going against what others think, to dare to say more clearly what appears to be the case, not all of soul, not even of our soul, descended, but something of it is permanently in the intelligible. But if what is in the sensible [world] dominates, or rather is dominated and in turmoil, it does not allow us to be aware of the things contemplated by the part of soul above. (IV. 8 [6]. 8. 1–6)

Plotinus' original idea that part of us remains in the intelligible (an idea generally rejected by the Platonists who came after him) suggests that we are permanently linked to a sort of transcendent consciousness which can be hidden by our present preoccupations. The return to the life of divine intellect is always available to us. It requires only that we change the focus of our lives, the level at which we are acting, making it coincide with the life of divine intellect.

The dynamic structure of our nature can be traced further back to the existence of soul as an activity and contemplation (through intellect) of the One. Soul is not something fixed and solid. It is a life simultaneously coming from and turning to the One. We exist as movement towards the One. Our very nature is a motion of 'assimilation to god'. To live according to our nature is then to seek to transcend ourselves, to divinize ourselves. This means living as divine intellect, which is how Plotinus describes happiness in a treatise dealing with the subject (I. 4 [46]).

It is clear that the movement of divinization cannot stop here. The One remains the ultimate goal of all aspiration, the ultimate object of desire. The movement that is our nature is completely fulfilled only in union with the One. This final felicity and the path that leads to it are described in one of Plotinus' finest writings, VI. 9 [9].

2. The Return to the One

Plotinus often refers to the methods and problems involved in attaining union with the One. For the sake of convenience we might distinguish three stages in reaching this goal: (1) the return to one's true self as soul; (2) attaining the life of divine intellect; (3) union with the One.

1. Starting from what is likely to be the position of many of us, Plotinus seeks to remind us of what we are. Reaching this insight presupposes that we are in control of our bodily passions, a control achieved through the practice of what Plotinus calls the 'civic' virtues (I. 2 [19]. 1–2), that is, the virtues of wisdom, courage, moderation, and justice as defined by Plato in the *Republic* (4. 428b–444a). This control allows us to detach ourselves mentally from material preoccupations (I. 2. 3–6: this detachment corresponds to the purificatory virtues mentioned in the *Phaedo*, 69bc) so that we discover our selves as soul, a divine reality independent of body and prior to it, which makes body and gives it its goodness and beauty. We are led on the path to this self-discovery by arguments (such as those summarized above in Ch. 1) showing the constitution of the world and its origin in soul:

Therefore there must be a two-part explanation given to those who are disposed in this way, if one will turn them toward opposite things and things which are first and lead them up to the highest and one and first. What then are these [two] parts? One shows the little value of the things that soul now values—this we will do at greater length elsewhere [Plotinus does not seem to have done this in the *Enneads*]—the other teaches and reminds soul of her origin and worth. (V. 1 [10]. 1. 22–8)

Thus Plotinus' arguments about the distinction between soul and body, the dependence of body on soul, are not merely arguments: they are methods for bringing the soul back to itself. 'And the ways whereby this was demonstrated were a kind of leading up' (I. 3 [20]. 1. 5–6). Soul's forgetfulness of itself in the material world is not a simple oversight on its part; it is a degradation of its life in so far as knowledge is a higher kind of life for it. To bring soul to know itself is to transform its life, to bring it to focus its life at a level close to the Good. To know is to live at a higher level.

2. The arguments lead us even further. They not only show soul what it is; they also lead it to see that the knowledge it has is derivative, that it derives from a higher form of thinking, the divine intellect which, unlike it, does not need to work through long logical processes, but possesses knowledge in a different and superior way (see above, Ch. 3). These arguments, like those bringing soul to self-discovery, are techniques of transformation of the self: the soul is put on the road to thinking in another way, that characteristic of divine intellect. It thus becomes intellect; it is what it now does.

Plotinus refers to this state of becoming divine intellect in a famous passage:

Many times, awakened to myself away from the body, becoming outside all else and within myself, seeing a wonderful and great beauty, believing myself then especially to be part of the higher realm, in act as the best life, having become one with the divine and based in it advancing to that activity, establishing myself above all other intelligible beings, then going down from this position in the divine, from intellect down to discursive reasoning, I am puzzled how I could ever, and now, descend, and how my soul has come to be in the body. (IV. 8 [6]. 1. 1–10)

Many readers (ancient and modern) have taken this text to refer to an experience of union with the One that Plotinus would have experienced a number of times. However, the expression 'many times' at the beginning of the passage relates, not to a number of experiences of union, but to a number of states of perplexity ('Many times . . . I am puzzled . . . ').[1] Furthermore the actual experience described in this passage is that of union with intellect. It is the force of habit that brings us to assume that all experience of union in Plotinus is experience of union with the One and thus to read this passage as if it exemplified the latter.

It should be noted that if the transformation of our lives that comes with becoming intellect is facilitated by philosophical arguments, these arguments must also be left behind: they make use of logical processes and are not required in the perfect knowledge of intellect. The reader of the *Enneads* must put these arguments aside on outgrowing their use.

3. This applies even more to the last stage, union with the One. The reasoning that brings us to self-knowledge as souls and points the way to becoming intellect can play no role in the ultimate step of union with the One. Reasoning can even get in the way of reaching a form of life above reasoning. As the One is beyond all knowledge and language (see above, Ch. 5), Plotinus can say little about union with it:

Therefore 'it cannot be said' or 'written', he says [Plato, *Letter* 7, 341c], but we speak and write, sending on to it and wakening from words [or explanations] towards contemplation, as if showing the way to him who wishes to see something. For teaching extends to the road and the passage, but the vision is the work of him who has decided to see. (VI. 9 [9]. 4. 11–16)

Plotinus can only recommend purification of oneself as intellect, the removal of all obstacles or differences that might separate us from the One (VI. 9. 7; see I. 6. 9), a waiting in silence (see VI. 7 [38]. 34). To visualize what happens we can refer to the initiation ceremonies

[1] Compare the standard phrase 'Many times I have wondered', which is used as a stylistic device for beginning a book or section (as in our Plotinian passage) in, for example, Xenophon, *Memorabilia* 1. 1 or in Marcus Aurelius, *Meditations*, 12. 4.

of the Greek mystery cults (VI. 9. 11). But such comparisons are inadequate:

> Therefore analogies teach, as do negations and knowledge of what comes from it [the One], and certain steps upwards. But what conveys us are purifications, virtues, and setting in order, and approaches to the intelligible, establishing ourselves there and feasting in what is there. Whoever has himself become contemplator and object contemplated, both of himself and of the others, becoming being and intellect and the 'complete living animal' [Plato, *Timaeus*, 31b], no longer looks outside; having become this he is near, and the next is it [the One], already shining in proximity on all the intelligible. Now leaving behind all learning, educated up and established in the beautiful, in which he is, up to this stage he thinks. But carried out by the wave, as it were, of intellect itself, lifted up high by it as it swells, so to speak, he suddenly saw, not seeing how, but the sight, filling the eyes with light, does not make him see another through itself, but the light itself was the sight seen. (VI. 7. 36. 6–21)

The union with the One raises a number of difficult questions, particularly if we wish to compare it with various types of religious mystical experience. As compared for example with the experience of Christian mystics, union with the One might be thought to entail annihilation of the self, whereas in the Christian version the distinction between creator and creature must remain, whatever the intensity of the experience of unification. If such issues merit a much more extensive discussion than can be attempted here, it might at least be noted that Plotinus himself does not think that the total union of the self with the One entails the annihilation of the self (see VI. 7. 34).

3. Philosophy and Mysticism

One can find in VI. 9 and elsewhere in Plotinus much of the vocabulary, imagery, and methods that appear later in the writings of great Christian mystics, Gregory of Nyssa, Augustine, Pseudo-Dionysius, Meister Eckhardt, John of the Cross, Jacob Boehme, to name but a few. Should we then describe Plotinus as a 'pagan mystic'? What is the importance of 'mystical experience' for his philosophy? In what sense can he, in view of this experience, be called a philosopher? As these questions easily lead to ambiguity and confusion, it might be useful to approach them with the following suggestions in mind:

1. It would seem reasonable to discuss Plotinus' standing as a philosopher in relation, not to standards incorporated by a modern (albeit unwilling) academic philosopher such as Wittgenstein, but to those represented by other ancient philosophers.

2. Plotinus' use of his experience of the world and of argumentation is comparable to that common in ancient philosophy, sometimes as good and sometimes as bad.

3. He regards the analysis of experience and logical reasoning as indispensable. For him there is no religious short-cut to union with the One. We must do philosophy and must reach the goal of philosophy, true and full understanding, before union with the One becomes possible.

4. If indispensable, reasoning is not enough. It is a means, not an end in itself. It is a movement, a form of desire leading to a life beyond itself.

5. In using experience of the world and reasoning as methods for transforming our lives, Plotinus pursues a purpose characteristic of ancient philosophy. Knowledge is also put in the service of changing our lives by Socrates, Plato, the Stoics, and Epicurus. Even the Sceptics, who denied the possibility of knowledge, regarded this denial as life-transforming. And Aristotle, whose *Nicomachean Ethics* begins with man's universal desire for happiness, tries to give us there the means for attaining this goal, and in the *Metaphysics*, which begins with man's universal desire for knowledge, he sets out to sketch the highest form of knowledge the complete possession of which would represent divine felicity.

6. Plotinus speaks of union with the One so convincingly that it seems unreasonable to doubt that he himself had experience of this union. This experience is clearly a powerful force animating his writing. Can this experience be described as 'religious', an experience of god to which he gives philosophical

clothing in his treatises? This question requires careful treatment. The experience of the One is the culmination of a series of experiences going from that of the material world to those of self-knowledge in soul and in intellect. Experience and reasoning are not opposed. Reasoning is a form of life, of experience, which produces union with the One, and this union is expressed in turn in reasoning. As regards religion, Plotinus' attitude can be gauged from his hostility to Gnosticism and his refusal to join Amelius and Porphyry in dabbling in various cults and rituals (above, Introduction s. 1). However he was prepared, as had been Plato, Aristotle, and the Stoics before him, to find in traditional (pagan) religion a popular expression of truths which he as a philosopher and follower of Plato wished to explain (for an example see II. 9. 9. 26–43).

The above points are intended to help in avoiding anachronisms, particularly the application of inappropriate modern dichotomies ('mystical' versus 'rational', 'experience' versus 'thought'), and to give a sense of Plotinus' own viewpoint. As such they might provide a basis for discussion of the questions raised at the beginning of this section.

4. The Ethics of Escape and the Ethics of Giving

The subject of Plotinus' 'mysticism' includes a further issue that requires attention. In pursuit of union with the One Plotinus advocates a rather ascetic, otherworldly attitude: we must turn away and escape from this material world, withdrawing ourselves from any involvement with it so as to be able to lead a transcendent life, that of intellect and that of the One. His is an ethics of escape from the world (see above, s. 2). In this respect, we might conclude, Plotinus is not faithful to Plato, who is concerned with improving our present lives, elaborating for this purpose a political philosophy in the *Republic* and in the *Laws*. However, Plotinus' ethics of escape leaves no room for politics. Plotinus, W. Theiler has said, is Plato diminished, a 'Plato without politics'.[2]

---

[2] W. Theiler, 'Plotin zwischen Platon und Stoa', in *Les Sources de Plotin*, Entretiens sur l'antiquité classique 5 (Geneva, 1960), 67.

This is only partially true. It is true that we do not find in Plotinus, as we do in Plato and Aristotle, extensive discussion of political structures, real and ideal, as contexts in which the human good may be realized. Plotinus recalls the civic virtues of Plato's *Republic* (above, s. 2). But the attention which he gives to political questions is minimal if compared, for example, to his discussion of issues in metaphysics and psychology. However, it does not follow from this that Plotinus' attitude is purely otherworldly, having no political application. The following remarks might serve to show this more clearly.

We should keep in mind that Plotinus' works are presumably directed towards a readership for whom an ethics of escape is appropriate and desirable, readers who are unclear about themselves, about their purpose in life, about the true object of their desire. If, having read the *Enneads*, such a reader successfully reaches union with the One, then another ethics becomes relevant, what we might call an ethics of giving:

abandoning external things [soul] must turn entirely to what is internal . . . ignoring . . . even itself, coming to be in the vision of it [the One], being with it, and having been sufficiently in company, as it were, with it, must come to tell, if it can, to another the life together there, a life perhaps such as Minos enjoyed, being said thus [Plato, *Parmenides*, 138e] to be the 'friend of Zeus', a life he recalled making laws as images of it, inspired by the contact with the divine to legislate. Or thinking political affairs as not worthy of himself, he wishes to remain always above. (VI. 9. 7. 17–28)

The vision of the One (the Good) *may* (but need not) lead to the desire to communicate the Good and this can be done both on the political level (lawgiving in the image of the Good) and on the individual level through the example of wisdom and virtue that can be given to others (see I. 2 [19]. 6. 8–12).

Porphyry refers to Plotinus' unrealized project to found an ideal city, Platonopolis (see above, Introduction s. 1). But Porphyry's *Life* suggests that Plotinus was active almost entirely on the individual level, as a model and guide for his friends and followers. We may regard his activity of teaching and of writing as aspects of this ethics of giving. If the *Enneads* propose an ethics of escape to the reader, they are themselves the product of an ethics of giving.

We might note finally that these two ethics recall two movements which are fundamental in Plotinus, those of soul as a cosmic force which organizes and perfects things ('giving') in function of detachment from them and orientation to the One ('escape'), and those of reality in general which is constituted by an activity of 'overflowing' from the One and turning back to the One. These two movements are not normally separated; they are two aspects of the one dynamic process which produces everything. They have become separated in some souls, however. These souls', our souls', loss of orientation towards the One requires a corrective movement, escape. This escape and the fulfilment of our desire of union with the One may be accompanied by a more balanced activity, the care and improvement of our lives and of the world in the light of wisdom.

Epilogue
Plotinus in Western Thought

In contrast to a number of their colleagues in continental Europe,
philosophers in England and North America have tended in general
for most of this century to dismiss Plotinus as an irrational mystic or
esoteric metaphysician, a marginal and negligible figure in the
Western intellectual tradition. This attitude, which is now changing,
derives in part from simple ignorance of Plotinus' works and of
history, in part from a narrow view which chooses to notice only
certain aspects of the past, in part from a restrictive and intolerant
philosophical stance which can allow no room for anything that
appears to be metaphysical. To these prejudices have been added
various clichés about Plotinus, inherited wittingly or unwittingly
from Christian polemic, for instance that he is a 'pantheist', that his
god produces by necessity and not freely (see above, Ch. 6 s. 4), that
this production is emanation in the literal sense. Contemporary work
on Plotinus ought to make it more difficult for such misrepresenta-
tions to continue to be taken seriously. Modern research has also
shown that Plotinus' philosophy is of considerable importance to the
history of Western culture. It might be useful to survey briefly here
some of the results of this research.

1. Elements of a History of the *Enneads* and Their Influence

It appears that Plotinus' school in Rome did not survive his death.
However, Porphyry did his best to promote the works of his teacher,
publishing not only the biography and edition (*Life of Plotinus* and
Enneads) but also summaries of and commentaries on the treatises as

well as an introductory manual (the *Sentences*) largely excerpted from the *Enneads*. Porphyry's pupil Iamblichus, who founded a successful philosophical school in Syria, vigorously criticized both Porphyry and Plotinus. If he brought new ideas and a new direction to ancient philosophy, his version of Platonism still owes its philosophical foundation to Plotinus. Iamblichus inspired a school of philosophers in Athens whose most important member, Proclus (who died in 485), paid Plotinus an exceptional tribute in writing a commentary on the *Enneads* (a few fragments of this survive). Teachers trained in the Athenian school gave new impetus in turn to Neoplatonic philosophy in the city where Plotinus had once studied, Alexandria. The Athenian school was eventually silenced in 529 by what had long been a Christian imperial state, but some of its more illustrious members, after a brief exile in Persia, continued to write and may even have been able, it is now thought, to carry on the school tradition well into the Muslim era in the border town of Harran. The Alexandrian Neoplatonists, some of whom were Christians, managed to continue teaching beyond 529 for another century.

We are now reaching a better appreciation of the extraordinary vitality and diversity of the Neoplatonic schools of Syria, Athens, and Alexandria. They are the last great movement in the history of ancient philosophy. If they had sources of inspiration other than Plotinus, his coherent and compelling interpretation of Plato, his successful appropriation of Aristotelian and Stoic ideas, his achievement of a synthesis containing many far-reaching implications as well as numerous difficulties and dilemmas, all this gave them both a substantial basis of reflection and the flexibility to evolve in various directions. Through these schools Plotinus influenced the birth of philosophy in the Byzantine and Islamic worlds and in the Latin West of the Middle Ages and the Renaissance. The indispensable point of departure for philosophical reflection in these periods and places was access to ancient Greek philosophy. This access was provided and shaped by Neoplatonism: Plato and Aristotle were read in the form in which they had been incorporated in the curriculum of the Neoplatonic schools and as accompanied by Neoplatonic commentaries. It is only comparatively recently, in the last century, that the effort has been undertaken to dispense with the mediation of Plotinus and his successors, to read Plato and Aristotle independently.

But let us return to the period of late antiquity in order to consider the influence exerted by Plotinus outside the philosophical schools. Philosophy represented during this period the highest level of education and most well-educated Christian theologians were familiar with the work of the dominant philosophical movement, Neoplatonism, and of its founder, Plotinus. The *Enneads* were read and quoted by leading theologians writing in Greek such as Eusebius of Caesarea, Basil the Great, and Gregory of Nyssa, and by those writing in Latin, Ambrose and Augustine. Augustine first read Plotinus as a young man in the 380s in the Latin translation made some decades earlier by a Roman professor of rhetoric, Marius Victorinus. This reading changed Augustine's life: it opened the way for his conversion to Christianity and had at first a major impact on his thought. When he became a bishop and a very powerful Church leader, he sought to restrict more and more this Plotinian influence. However the words that consoled him in his last days, so his biographer Possidius reports, were those of Plotinus (*Enn*. I. 4. 7. 24–5). Indeed much of Christian theology, as it developed in late antiquity, shows Plotinus' influence: the strong emphasis on the incorporeality of the divine and its immaterial omnipresence (see above, Ch. 2 s. 5); the stress on man's soul, man's inner self, and on return to one's self and to God through an internalizing moral and mental ascent; the explanation of evil as a lack of good, as a turning away from the good (see above, Ch. 8); the vision of all reality as coming from and returning to God. At the same time Christian writers sought to subordinate Plotinus to their religion or rejected him outright, as he did not share central doctrines of faith: the Trinity, the incarnation, crucifixion, and resurrection of Christ, the necessity of grace (see Augustine, *Confessions*, 7. 9).

Plotinus was read by many prominent intellectuals in Byzantium, the eastern half of the Roman Empire which survived up to the Turkish capture of Constantinople in 1453. The most influential of them, the philosopher and statesman Michael Psellus, made Plotinus a fashionable author in the eleventh century. He used many excerpts from the *Enneads* and also read Proclus' commentary on the *Enneads*. Enthusiasm for pagan wisdom was politically dangerous in a state whose identity was so closely bound to the Christian religion: Psellus was careful to distance himself from his pagan sources, but some of his followers did not escape persecution. Other Byzantine scholars preferred Aristotle, on religious and philosophical grounds, and criticized Plotinus. We owe our earliest manuscript copies of the *Enneads* to the devotion of Byzantine scholars and copyists of the twelfth and thirteenth centuries. On the eve of the collapse of Byzantium, another scholar and philosopher, Pletho, saw in pagan religion (Neoplatonized) a last desperate hope for his Hellenic culture, but it was Italian humanists who profited from the Greek manuscripts (including Plotinus) collected by Pletho's pupil Bessarion when he settled in Italy after the council of Florence (1438).

Further east, in the medieval Islamic world, Plotinus enjoyed the 'power of anonymity' (F. Rosenthal's phrase): he was scarcely known by name but well known by his works. Arabic paraphrases of *Enneads* IV–VI[1] circulated in various forms: as a 'Theology of Aristotle' (used by the philosophers Al-Kindi, Al-Farabi, and Avicenna, among others); as a 'Letter of Divine Science'; and as passages cited by various authors as the work of a 'Greek old man [or sage]'. One of the two versions of the 'Theology of Aristotle' survives in Arabic texts written in Hebrew characters and there are other indications of the use of the 'Theology' by Jewish writers living in the Islamic world.

In contrast to their Byzantine and Islamic contemporaries, medieval Western thinkers had no direct knowledge of the *Enneads*. Marius Victorinus' Latin translation did not survive beyond the period of late antiquity and no other translation of Plotinus was attempted in the West before the fifteenth century. However, a good deal of Plotinus was available in the form of references, quotations, excerpts, and adaptations in the writings of Ambrose, of Augustine, and of another late antique (pagan) writer, Macrobius. Thus medieval thinkers such as Thomas Aquinas were aware of Plotinus'

---

[1] Conveniently available in English in *Plotini opera*, ed. P. Henry and H.-R. Schwyzer (Brussels, 1959), vol. ii.

identity and importance and felt in a position to discuss him, albeit at second hand. This filtered presence of Plotinus was strengthened by the popularity in the Middle Ages of two late antique Christian authors inspired by the Neoplatonic schools of Athens and Alexandria, Boethius and the mysterious Christian pupil of Proclus to whom we refer today as 'Pseudo-Dionysius'. By reading these authors, Western medieval Platonists such as John Scotus Eriugena had indirect access to Plotinian ideas, even if they had no first-hand knowledge of the *Enneads*.

We know of the presence of copies of the *Enneads* among the Greek manuscripts collected by scholars and humanists in Italy in the first half of the fifteenth century. Like their medieval predecessors they were aware of Plotinus' importance. But they could also quote directly from his treatises, Francesco Filelfo in 1467, Argyropoulos already in 1457. When Marsilio Ficino began work near Florence in the 1460s on his great Latin translation of Plato he read the *Enneads* (he regarded Plotinus as a Plato *redivivus*), annotating two Greek manuscripts of Plotinus and compiling excerpts and summaries. His writings of the 1460s and 1470s (*Commentary on the Symposium, Platonic Theology*) show his thorough knowledge of the *Enneads*. In 1484, on finishing his work on Plato, he turned to translating and commenting on Plotinus. He claims that the impulse to do this came from Giovanni Pico della Mirandola. But reading Plato as he did in Neoplatonic terms, he must have had the idea long before. His Latin translation of the *Enneads*, accompanied by a commentary, was printed in 1492. It was a magnificent achievement. Almost four centuries would pass before a new translation was felt to be necessary and it is still consulted by scholars today. In making Plotinus and other Neoplatonist authors available in Latin, Ficino was proposing to his contemporaries a philosophy which he felt was compatible with Christianity in a way that Aristotelianism was not: the medieval synthesis of Aristotelian philosophy and Christian faith had become increasingly more fragile as intensified study of Aristotle inspired challenges to the Christian doctrines of the beginning of the world and the survival of the human soul after death. Ficino's Plotinus was very well received by humanists in Italy, France, Spain, and England. In 1519 Plotinus made another (disguised) appearance, when a Latin version of the Arabic 'Theology of Aristotle' was published. As such it was included in a number of sixteenth-century editions of Aristotle. If its attribution to Aristotle was often doubted (for example by Martin Luther), its true Plotinian origin was not established until 1812. In 1580 the first printed edition of the Greek text of the *Enneads* was published.

The international success of Ficino's revival of Platonic philosophy in the sixteenth century was followed in the next two centuries by a decline in which Plotinus shared. Among the factors responsible for this were the growth of secular rationalism (Ficino had linked Plotinus to Christian religion); theological rejection of the Platonizing of Christian faith; and scholarly rejection of the Neoplatonic approach to reading Plato. Plotinus found favour, however, in some quarters: his works were read and used in the seventeenth century by the Cambridge Platonists Ralph Cudworth and Henry More, and in the eighteenth century his ideas attracted the attention and admiration of Berkeley and (at the end of the century) of Goethe, Schelling, and Hegel. Hegel's colleague F. Creuzer published two treatises of Plotinus that were close to the interests of German Idealist philosophy, *Enneads* III. 8 and I. 6, and was aware of the timeliness of the new complete edition of Plotinus which he published with G. Moser in 1835. He was followed by a long and distinguished series of German scholars who edited, translated, and interpreted Plotinus. A French contemporary and admirer of Hegel, Victor Cousin, inspired a similar tradition of Neoplatonic scholarship in France, which would prepare the ground for Henri Bergson's fruitful encounter with the *Enneads*. In nineteenth-century England Thomas Taylor's English translations and the Hegelian movement would bring Plotinus to the attention of Wordsworth, Blake, Coleridge, and Yeats. In this atmosphere Stephan MacKenna gave up a successful career in journalism in order to devote his life—it would be a life of great hardship—to translating Plotinus into English. When his translation was published (1917–30) it was greeted as a literary masterpiece.

2. Plotinus' Presence

Plotinus' presence in Western culture extends well beyond the circle of those who read the *Enneads*. The diffusion of his ideas through such influential intermediaries as Augustine and Ficino ensured a much wider impact, affecting not only the history of philosophy, but also the history of religious thought, literature, and art. Theologians, writers, and poets have been mentioned above and the significance of Plotinus' ideas for the theory of art and of artistic activity as well as for the history of mysticism has been noted in earlier chapters (above, Ch. 9 s. 2, Ch. 10 ss. 2–3).

It is clear that different intellectual movements in different periods and places found Plotinus' ideas appealing in various ways. If we wish to survey aspects of Plotinus' philosophy that may be of particular interest in the context of modern philosophical reflection, we might begin by selecting some examples from the ideas and theories which have been discussed in earlier parts of this book. The following selection is not intended to be comprehensive: it could easily be expanded and adjusted, depending on one's particular interests and preferences.

As a first example I would mention the internalization of intelligible reality in Plotinus (see above, Ch. 1 s. 6). In thinking about the two worlds of Platonism, the sensible and the intelligible worlds, Plotinus invites us to discover intelligible being as within soul, as within us. The fundamental structures and sources of reality are to be sought in our innermost nature. Or, as Plotinus might prefer to say (standing conventional expressions on their head), the world is in soul, as soul is in intellect and intellect in the One.

Of interest in this connection is the way in which Plotinus, in approaching the two-world distinction as (at first) a soul/body distinction, formulates the difference between soul and body with great clarity and rigour (above, Ch. 1). In clarifying this difference, he also has much to say about how these two realities might relate to each other (above, Ch. 2).

Plotinus has many new things to say about an area that is little discussed in ancient philosophy, the area of human subjectivity. He reminds us that in philosophical enquiry there is not only the object being investigated, but also the someone who is investigating. We want to understand the world so as to understand ourselves. Plotinus introduces for the first time a philosophy of the self, its multiple levels, its mobility, its roots in a permanent thought that becomes unconscious through our preoccupation with external things (above, Ch. 10). Plotinus tries to speak to our inner selves as we search for insight. His words can take on a direct, personal, informal quality which is universal in appeal: differences in sex and culture (Greek, barbarian) do not have the importance they have in Plato and Aristotle. The cosmopolitanism of the Roman Empire, the cosmic citizenship advocated by the Stoics, have become in Plotinus the universal transcendent sisterhood of souls (see IV. 3. 6. 10–14) to which we all belong.

We might add here also his interest in the limitations of thought and language (above, Ch. 5). He is acutely aware of how human rationality and its expression in language are limited with respect to some of the realities under investigation. This awareness is matched by an adventurous and entirely individual use of the Greek language that pushes at its limits, inventing new words and bending grammar with sometimes startling freedom.

In a curious way some of what Plotinus says points to the future. His metaphysics of the world—soul organizing the world—seems, on the face of it, irremediably outdated. Yet our impact on the world is now such that we are making ourselves into the organizers of nature. We are becoming Plotinian souls: we can manage things with wisdom or allow ourselves to be driven by unlimited, chaotic, and self-destructive desire. Of course Plotinus does not think that we can simply invent the wisdom on the basis of which life can be led successfully: in his view we must derive it from divine intellect. However, we are faced with such problems that we cannot avoid the necessity of developing this wisdom, a wisdom that goes beyond divisions of sex, nation, race, and culture and that relates to human nature as a whole; that does not make the mistake of substituting uniformity for unity; that is not parochial, as are the political ideals of Plato and Aristotle, but that sees humanity and all nature as a unity in diversity, an example (but not, perhaps, the ideal paradigm) of which might be the unity in diversity of divine intellect in Plotinus.

Plotinus' intellectual attitude is also a challenge that we face. He describes the kind of philosophy that he wishes to cultivate as follows: 'The form of philosophy which is sought by us . . . shows simplicity of character combined with purity of reflection, striving after dignity, not presumption, being courageous with reason and much care, precaution, and circumspection' (II. 9. 14. 37–43). Plotinus' writing comes close to displaying these qualities. He shows an intellectual rigour which is aware of its limits and does not claim a monopoly on insight, a comprehensive view of things which is open and flexible, sensitive to the dynamism of life.

Guide to Further Reading

What follows contains suggestions (by no means exhaustive) for further reading in and around Plotinus' *Enneads*. The suggestions are grouped corresponding to each of the chapters of this book, and are of three kinds:

1. references to *other* texts of Plotinus and of other ancient philosophers relevant to the matter discussed in the chapter;
2. references to selected studies by modern authors of this material;
3. references to themes in Plotinus related to the problems examined in the chapter.

I hope in this way to provide the reader with means for going beyond what is discussed in this book. The Bibliography given below (s. 6) gives details of publications which are indicated here only by the name of the author (and the item number in the Bibliography, if more than one work of the author is listed there).

Information on editions and translations of Plotinus can be found in the Bibliography. Excellent introductory surveys of Plotinus are provided by Armstrong (3), 195–263, and by Hadot (3). Rist (6) offers challenging discussion of a wide range of philosophical issues. Blumenthal (2) is an essential monograph on the theory of soul. The most important and thorough scholarly survey of Plotinus is Schwyzer (1). A useful systematic guide to themes in the *Enneads* can be found in R. Harder, R. Beutler, and W. Theiler, *Plotins Schriften* (Hamburg, 1956–71), vi. 103–72.

Introduction: Plotinus' Life and Works

Porphyry's *Life of Plotinus* can be found at the beginning of every complete edition or translation of Plotinus. Very detailed information on a number of aspects of the *Life* can be found in Brisson *et al.*, including questions of chronology which are also discussed by Igal (1).

Some impression of the history of the Roman Empire in the third century can be obtained from the *Cambridge Ancient History*, vol. xii (in particular ch. 6), Rémondon, and de Blois. The intellectual and spiritual climate is portrayed in Festugière and Dodds (3). Jerphagnon is a provocative study of Plotinus' political involvements.

For Plotinus' attitude to and use of Plato see Matter, Charrue, Szlezák. Dillon is a useful source of information on the Middle Platonists, many of whom are described in important articles in Dörrie. See also Donini. On Ammonius Sakkas see Schwyzer (2), Schroeder (3). For the Aristotelian commentators see Gottschalk, Sharples, and the major work by Moraux. For Hellenistic philosophy (Stoicism, Epicureanism, Scepticism) see Long (1), an excellent introductory survey, and the very useful two-volume collection of documents in Long and Sedley which should be consulted on all aspects of Hellenistic philosophy touched on in this book (vol. i prints the documents in English translation with some explanation; vol. ii gives the Greek and Latin originals with detailed discussion and bibliography). Rudolph provides an up-to-date introduction to Gnosticism; or see the older book by Jonas (1). The Nag Hammadi texts are translated in Robinson, and compared in detail with Plotinian texts by Elsas.

Chapter 1. Soul and Body

1. For Stoic and Epicurean discussions of immortality, see Long and Sedley i. 318 (Stoicism), 66, 69–70 (Epicureanism). For the Stoic concept of soul, see Long and Sedley, i. 313–19. An Aristotelian attack on Stoic materialism can be found in Alexander of Aphrodisias, *De anima*, 17. 9–20. 26, a Platonic attack in Alcinous, *Didaskalikos*, ch. 11. See also Atticus, fragment 7, Numenius, fragment 4a. For further texts on soul, see *Enneads* IV. 2 [4]; IV. 9 [8]; IV. 1 [21]; VI. 1 [42]. 26–7 (on soul and body); I. 1 [53] (on soul and body with specific reference to man); and below section 3. On body see also below, on Chapter 7 (s. 3).

2. For analysis and further bibliography concerning Aristotle's theory of soul, see Nussbaum and Rorty. The Stoic concept of soul is discussed by Long (2). Plotinus' distinction between soul and body is examined in general terms by Rich (3) and Blumenthal (2), ch. 2. Van Straaten deals with the polemic with Stoicism in *Ennead* IV. 7 which is also assessed, as is the polemic with Aristotle, by Blumenthal (2). More generally on Plotinus' debt to Stoicism see Graeser. Emilsson (1), 145–8 compares Plotinus with Descartes.

3. Many aspects of soul as it relates to body are discussed at considerable length in *Ennead* IV. 3–5 [27–9]: the descent and presence of soul (both cosmic and individual) in body, the various psychic functions (in particular

memory and sense-perception). (On sight see also II. 8 [35], IV. 6 [41].) For all of this see Blumenthal (2) and, as regards perception, Emilsson (1).

Chapter 2. The Relation between Sensible and Intelligible Reality

1. See also *Enneads* III. 6 [26]. 6; IV. 3 [27]. 20–3; V. 5 [32]. 9.
2. On Plotinus' solution in VI. 4–5 see O'Meara (3) and, more recently, Corrigan. (A philosophical commentary on VI. 4–5 is being prepared by E. Emilsson and S. Strange.) O'Meara (5) discusses in more detail the question of soul's action on body. On presence as dependence see also Arnou (2), 167–72. On the world as dependent image of the intelligible see Armstrong (10).
3. For the Stoic theory that one body can permeate another and yet stay unified (*krasis di' holou*) see Plotinus, *Ennead* II. 7 [37]; Alexander of Aphrodisias, *De mixtione*. If body does not change soul, soul still experiences moral and mental changes, on which see III. 6 [26]. 1–5.

Chapter 3. Soul, Intellect, and the Forms

1. On truth see also *Ennead* VI. 6 [34]. 6; on intelligible reality see the detailed study in VI. 2 [43] (where Plotinus interprets the five 'greatest kinds' of Plato's *Sophist*, 254e, as concerning the structure of the intelligible).
2. For the debate concerning the relation between intellect and the Forms in Middle Platonism and Neoplatonism see Pépin (1), Frede, and (with particular reference to Plotinus) Armstrong (2). On the ignorant maker of the world in Gnosticism see Rudolph, 67–87. For Sceptic philosophy see Long (1) and the texts in Long and Sedley; for Plotinus' response to Scepticism see Wallis (2) and Emilsson (3). The theory of a non-discursive form of thinking is debated by Lloyd (1), Sorabji, ch. 10, and Alfino. Discursive thinking in Plotinus is discussed by Blumenthal (2), ch. 8; on the judgement of sense-data in terms of norms derived from intellect see Blumenthal (2), ch. 8, Blumenthal (5), and Emilsson (1), 134–7.
3. On the range of Forms see also *Enneads* V. 9 [5]. 9–14; VI. 7 [38]. 1–11; on Forms of individuals see V. 9. 12; V. 7 [18]; Rist (4), Blumenthal (1) (= Blumenthal (2), ch. 9), Armstrong (6). On the structure of the intelligible world see Hadot (1). For the place of numbers in the intelligible see *Ennead* VI. 6 [34] with the commentary by Bertier, Brisson, *et al.*

Chapter 4. Intellect and the One

1. See also *Enneads* V. 1 [10]. 5; III. 9 [13]. 9; III. 8 [30]. 8–11; V. 5 [32]. 4–5; VI. 7 [38]. 13–14, 37–42; V. 3 [49]. 10–12, 16. (Some of these texts are discussed by Bussanich.) For the highest principle as both simple and intellect in Middle Platonism see, in addition to Alcinous, Numenius, fragments 11, 15–17, 19–20.

2. For a comparison between Plotinus' One and Aristotle's god see Rist (7). The documents concerning Plato's 'oral teaching' can be found in Gaiser or Richard (Cherniss (1) argues for scepticism concerning the notion of an esoteric oral teaching). Emilsson (1), ch. 1, restates the argument from unity of VI. 9. For thinking as a form of desire see Arnou (2), ch. 3, part IV. Rist (5) and Whittaker (1), essay XI, compare Plotinus' monism with anticipations of it in earlier Platonist and Pythagorean authors. Dodds (1) and Rist (3) discuss pre-Plotinian monistic readings of Plato's *Parmenides*. For Plotinus' metaphysical interpretation of the *Parmenides* see Charrue, ch. 1.

3. On the question whether the One, although beyond intellect, might have some form of consciousness or awareness of itself see *Enneads* V. 4 [7]. 2; VI. 9 [9]. 6; III. 9 [13]. 9; VI. 7 [38]. 41; V. 3 [49]. 10, 12–13; Rist (6), ch. 4.

Chapter 5. Speaking of the One

1. For philosophical and religious texts of the period concerning divine ineffability see Festugière, vol. iv (*Le Dieu inconnu*), esp. ch. 6; Mortley (2), vol. ii, ch. 1; Alcinous *Didaskalikos*, ch. 10; Numenius, fragments 2, 7. See also *Enneads* V. 5 [32]. 6, 13; VI. 7 [38]. 38; VI. 8 [39]. 8–9, 13.

2. For further analysis see Festugière, Whittaker (1), essays IX–XIII, Mortley (1), (2), vol. ii, ch. 3, Schroeder (1), and O'Meara (6). On the One as infinite see Rist (6), 25–30.

3. On Plotinus' concept of language, see Pépin (2), O'Meara (6), Alfino.

Chapter 6. The Derivation of All Things from the One (I)

1. See also *Enneads* III. 8 [30]. 8–11; V. 5 [32]. 7–8; VI. 7 [38]. 15–16, 35; V. 3 [49]. 11. On the theory of two activities see also IV. 5 [29]. 7; II. 9 [33].

8. On the 'dyad' considered as a sort of intelligible matter see II. 4 [12]. 2–5;

II. 5 [25]. 1–3. For the differences between soul, world-soul, and individual souls see IV. 3 [27]. 1–8; IV. 4 [28]. 13–14; II. 1 [40]. 5. On the unity of all souls see IV. 9 [8].

2. For the derivation of intellect see Atkinson's commentary on V. 1. 6–7, Bussanich's comments on some of the texts listed above, and, for some recent studies, Lloyd (2), Schroeder (2). On the 'dyad' as intelligible matter see Rist (2). On the different types of soul see Helleman-Elgersma's commentary on IV. 3. 1–8 and most especially Blumenthal (3). On the freedom of the One see Rist (6), ch. 6, Leroux's commentary on VI. 8, Kremer's very useful article, and O'Brien (2) (on the freedom or necessity of soul's descent to body).

Chapter 7. The Derivation of All Things from the One (II)

1. On the constitution of the world see also *Enneads* III. 6 [26]. 7–19 (with particular reference to matter); IV. 3 [27]. 9–11. The critique of a calculating demiurge can also be found in IV. 4 [28]. 9–13; V. 8 [31]. 7; VI. 7 [38]. 1–3; III. 2 [47]. 1–2; and, with specific reference to Gnosticism, in II. 9 [33]. 10–12. On nature see also IV. 4 [27]. 13–14; VI. 7 [38]. 7, 11; II. 3 [52]. 9, 17–18. On matter see also II. 4 [12]. 6–16; II. 5 [25]. 4–5.

2. For the debates in the Platonic tradition concerning the demiurge of the *Timaeus*, see Brisson, Baltes. For Plato, Aristotle, the Stoics, and Epicureans see Mansfeld (essay XIV). On the Gnostic demiurge see Quispel, i. 213–20, and, on Plotinus' criticism of it, O'Meara (4). The theory of contemplative making is well presented in Deck and Santa Cruz de Prunes and its influence on modern philosophy of nature is demonstrated by Hadot (2). For discussion of the view that for Plotinus matter is not generated, see O'Brien (1), (3), (4), (5), Corrigan. On time and eternity in Plotinus see Beierwaltes' commentary on III. 7.

3. On immanent qualities and forms in the sensible world see *Ennead* II. 6 [17]; Rist (6), ch. 8. On the sensible object see Emilsson (2). On the heavens see *Ennead* II. 2 [14]; II. 1 [40]. For critical (and quite technical) discussion of the Aristotelian and Stoic theories of categories as applied to the sensible world see VI. 1 [42] and VI. 3 [44]; Rutten, Wurm.

Chapter 8. Evil

1. See also *Enneads* II. 4 [12]. 16; III. 6 [26]. 11; IV. 3 [27]. 16; II. 9 [33]. 8–9, 12–13; VI. 7 [38]. 23, 28; I. 1 [53]. 12. On evil in Plato see Cherniss (2);

for the Middle Platonists see Numenius, fragment 52, and Armstrong (9). On evil in Gnosticism see Rudolph, 65–7.

2. On the question whether Plotinus has a coherent theory of evil see Fuller, Costello, Rist (6), ch. 9, Rist (1), (9), O'Brien (1), (2), (4). On the apostasy of soul see Baladi (1), (2); Jonas (2). For the relation between Plotinus and the Christian theologians Gregory of Nyssa and Augustine on the subject of evil see Daniélou, Rist (8). On transmigration of the soul see also *Ennead* III. 4 [15] and Rich (1).

3. On the relation between providence, fate, and free will see (in addition to *Ennead* III. 2–3) III. 1 [3]; VI. 8 [39]. 1–6; Rist (6), ch. 10. Plotinus attacks astrology in III. 1 [3] and II. 3 [52].

Chapter 9. Beauty

1. On beauty see also *Enneads* I. 3 [20]. 1–2; V. 8 [31]. 13; II. 9 [33]. 17; III. 5 [50]. 1.

2. On Plotinus' theory of beauty see Armstrong (5), (8), Moreau, Beierwaltes (3). For the critique of the theory of symmetry see Anton (1), Horn. On the relation between beauty and the Good see Rist (6), ch. 5. For the importance of Plotinus' concept of beauty for the Middle Ages and the Renaissance see Beierwaltes (3), Panofsky, Chastel.

3. On Plotinus' approach to art and artists see Rich (2), Anton (2), de Keyser.

Chapter 10. The Return of Soul: Philosophy and Mysticism

1. On human nature see *Enneads* VI. 7 [38]. 4–7; II. 3 [52]. 9; I. 1 [53]. On happiness see also I. 5 [36]; I. 7 [54]. 1–2. On the mobility of the self see III. 4 [15]; VI. 7 [38]. 6. For the ethics of ascent see I. 2 [19]; III. 6 [26]. 5; II. 9 [33]. 15. On the universal desire for the Good see V. 5 [32]. 12; VI. 2 [43]. 11; III. 2 [47]. 3. On union with the One see also V. 5 [32]. 8; V. 3 [49]. 17.

2. On human nature see Armstrong (3), 223–7, Igal (2). On happiness see Rist (6), ch. 11, Himmerich, Beierwaltes (4). On the concept of the self and its mobility see Hadot (3), ch. 2, O'Daly (1). For Plotinus' mysticism see Dodds (2), Rist (6), ch. 16, Arnou (1), (2), ch. 6, Beierwaltes (2), (5), 123–54, (6). Arguments for and against *Ennead* IV. 8. 1 as having to do with union with the One can be found in Rist (6), 195–7, Hadot (5), 14–16, and O'Meara (1); see also Merlan (on the Aristotelian concept of union with

divine intellect). The question of annihilation of the self in the One is treated in O'Daly (1), ch. 4, O'Daly (2). Armstrong (4) discusses the importance of experience of the One for Plotinus. For ancient philosophy as being directed to transforming lives see Hadot (4). Jerphagnon discusses some political aspects of Plotinus. Hadot (3), ch. 6, treats of Plotinus' moral role in his circle; see also Rist (6), ch. 12.

Epilogue: Plotinus in Western Thought

For further details and bibliography concerning the influence of Plotinus' *Enneads* see Schwyzer (1), 581–90, and O'Meara (7). On the Neoplatonic schools in general see Wallis (1), Armstrong (3), Beierwaltes (5). On Harran see I. Hadot (includes a summary of M. Tardieu's recent research). Plotinus' influence on Christian theologians and on later periods is discussed in Armstrong (7), Daniélou, Rist (8), Beierwaltes (7), 80–94, Beierwaltes (3), (4), Henry (1), (2), and in the conferences *Néoplatonisme* and *Plotino* (below, Bibliography, s. 4). On the 'Theology of Aristotle' see most recently Aouad. For Plotinus and German Idealism see Beierwaltes (1), 83–153, and Hadot (2). On the modern separation of Plato from Neoplatonic interpretation see Tigerstedt.

Bibliography

1. Editions and Translations of Plotinus

The authoritative critical edition of the Greek text of Plotinus was published in three volumes (vol. iii includes valuable indexes for ancient authors used by and using Plotinus) by P. Henry and H.-R. Schwyzer, *Plotini opera* (Brussels, 1951–73). They then published a study version of the edition (with revisions), also in three volumes: *Plotini opera*, ed. P. Henry and H. R. Schwyzer (Oxford, 1964–82). Access to the Greek text is given by an exhaustive word index: J. Sleeman and G. Pollet, *Lexicon Plotinianum* (Leiden 1980.)

Henry and Schwyzer's edition (with some revisions) is printed facing an excellent English translation in seven volumes by A. H. Armstrong, *Plotinus* (Cambridge, Mass., 1966–88.) Armstrong's translation supersedes that by S. MacKenna (*Plotinus: The Enneads*, rev. B. Page (3rd edn., London, 1956), reprinted in abridgement by Penguin Books with an introduction by J. Dillon, 1991), which, although a work of great literary quality, is less reliable and less clear. E. O'Brien, *The Essential Plotinus* (New York, 1964), translates *Enneads* I. 6, V. 9, IV. 8, VI. 9, V. 1, V. 2, I. 2, I. 3, IV. 3, III. 8.

2. Bibliographies

The bibliography given here and in the following sections is not intended to be complete. Full bibliographies of more recent work on Plotinus, with helpful introductions, have been published by H. Blumenthal, 'Plotinus in the Light of Twenty Years' Scholarship, 1951–1971', and by K. Corrigan and P. O'Cleirigh, 'The Course of Plotinian Scholarship from 1971 to 1986', in W. Haase and H. Temporini (eds.), *Aufstieg und Niedergang der römischen Welt (ANRW)*, ii. xxxvi. 1 (Berlin, 1987), 528–623.

3. Commentaries

Some commentaries on individual Plotinian treatises are now available:

III. 5: A. Wolters, *Plotinus 'On Eros'* (Toronto, 1984), and P. Hadot, *Plotin traité 50* (Paris, 1990).

III. 7: W. Beierwaltes, *Plotin über Ewigkeit und Zeit* (Frankfurt, 1967).

III. 8, V. 8, V. 5, II. 9: D. Roloff, *Plotin: Die Großschrift* (Berlin, 1971), and V. Cilento, *Paideia antignostica* (Florence, 1971).

IV. 3. 1–8: W. Helleman-Elgersma, *Soul-Sisters: A Commentary on Enneads IV. 3 (27), 1–8* (Amsterdam, 1980).

V. 1: M. Atkinson, *Ennead V. 1: On the Three Principal Hypostases* (Oxford, 1983).

V. 3: W. Beierwaltes, *Selbsterkenntnis und Erfahrung der Einheit* (Frankfurt, 1991), and H. Oosthout, *Modes of Knowledge and the Transcendental* (Amsterdam, 1991).

VI. 6: J. Bertier, L. Brisson, *et al.*, *Plotin: Traité sur les nombres* (Paris, 1980).

VI. 7: P. Hadot, *Plotin traité 38 (VI 7)* (Paris, 1988).

VI. 8: G. Leroux, *Plotin: Traité sur la liberté et la volonté de l'Un* (Paris, 1990).

For other treatises it is worth consulting the introductions to each treatise to be found in E. Bréhier, *Plotin: Les Ennéades* (Paris, 1924–38), and the notes in R. Harder, R. Beutler, and W. Theiler, *Plotins Schriften* (Hamburg, 1956–71) (which offers an excellent German translation and is exceptional in arranging Plotinus' treatises in chronological order). J. Igal's Spanish translation, *Porfirio: Vida de Plotino: Plotino Enéadas I–II, III–IV*, 2 vols. (Madrid, 1982, 1985), is also excellent and includes useful introductions and notes.

4. Conferences and Collections

Some of the best work on Plotinus has appeared in the papers of various conferences. Individual papers are listed below in section 6, where I refer to the conferences using the following abbreviations:

Néoplatonisme: *Le Néoplatonisme* (Colloque du CNRS) (Paris, 1971).

Plotino: *Plotino e il Neoplatonismo in Oriente e in Occidente* (Rome, 1974).
Sources: *Les Sources de Plotin* (Entretiens sur l'antiquité classique 5) (Geneva, 1960).

Many informative articles on Plotinus and especially on the various philosophical movements of the early centuries AD can be found in *ANRW*: W. Haase and H. Temporini (eds.), *Aufstieg und Niedergang der römischen Welt* (Berlin, 1987–90), II. xxxvi. 1, 2, 3, 4.

5. Some Middle Platonists and Aristotelians

For information on Plotinus' Middle Platonist and Aristotelian predecessors see the works, listed below in section 6, of Dillon, Whittaker (2), Donini, Gottschalk, Sharples, Moraux. I list here editions and translations of some Middle Platonist and Aristotelian texts which are mentioned in this book:

ALCINOUS [Albinus], *Didaskalikos*, ed. and French trans. by J. Whittaker and P. Louis, *Alkinoos: Enseignement des doctrines de Platon* (Paris, 1990).
ALEXANDER of Aphrodisias, *De anima*, ed. I. Bruns (Berlin, 1887).
——*De anima*, Eng. trans. (to be used with caution) by A. Fotinis (Washington, DC, 1979).
——*De fato*, ed. and Eng. trans. by R. Sharples, *Alexander of Aphrodisias: On Fate* (London, 1983).
——*De mixtione*, ed. and Eng. trans. by R. Todd, *Alexander of Aphrodisias on Stoic Physics* (Leiden, 1976).
——*On Aristotle's Metaphysics 1*, Eng. trans. by W. Dooley (London, 1989).
APULEIUS, *De Platone et eius dogmate*, in *Apulée: Opuscules philosophiques et fragments*, ed. and French trans. by J. Beaujeu (Paris, 1973).
ATTICUS, *Fragments*, ed. and French trans. by E. des Places (Paris, 1977).
NUMENIUS, *Fragments*, ed. and French trans. by E. des Places (Paris, 1973).

6. Select Bibliography
(For abbreviations see above, section 4)

ALFINO, M., 'Plotinus and the Possibility of Non-propositional Thought', *Ancient Philosophy*, 8 (1988), 273–84.
ANTON, J. (1), 'Plotinus' Refutation of Beauty as Symmetry', *Journal of Aesthetics and Art Criticism*, 23 (1964–5), 233–7.
——(2), 'Plotinus' Conception of the Functions of the Artist', *Journal of Aesthetics and Art Criticism*, 26 (1967–8), 91–101.

AOUAD, M., 'Aristote', in R. Goulet (ed.), *Dictionnaire des philosophes antiques* (Paris, 1989), i. 541–90.

ARMSTRONG, A. (1), *The Architecture of the Intelligible Universe in the Philosophy of Plotinus* (Cambridge, 1940). (On this book see Armstrong's new preface to the French translation, *L'Architecture de l'univers intelligible dans la philosophie de Plotin* (Ottawa, 1984), 11–15.)

——(2), 'The Background of the Doctrine "That the Intelligibles are not outside the Intellect" ', *Sources*, 393–413 = Armstrong (7), study IV.

——(3) (ed.), *The Cambridge History of Later Greek and Early Medieval Philosophy* (Cambridge, 1967).

——(4), 'Tradition, Reason and Experience in the Thought of Plotinus', *Plotino*, 171–94 = Armstrong (7), study XVII.

——(5), 'Beauty and the Discovery of Divinity in the Thought of Plotinus', in J. Mansfeld and L. de Rijk (eds.), *Kephalaion. Studies . . . Offered to C. J. de Vogel* (Assen, 1975), 155–63 = Armstrong (7), study XIX.

——(6), 'Form, Individual and Person', *Dionysius*, 1 (1977), 49–68 = Armstrong (7), study XX.

——(7), *Plotinian and Christian Studies* (London, 1979).

——(8), 'The Divine Enhancement of Earthly Beauties: The Hellenic and Platonic Tradition', *Eranos Jahrbuch*, 53 (1984), 49–81 = Armstrong (11), study IV.

——(9), 'Dualism Platonic, Gnostic, and Christian', in D. Runia (ed.), *Plotinus amid Gnostics and Christians* (Amsterdam, 1984), 29–52 = Armstrong (11), study XII.

——(10), 'Platonic Mirrors', *Eranos Jahrbuch*, 55 (1986), 147–81 = Armstrong (11), study VI.

——(11), *Hellenic and Christian Studies* (London, 1990).

ARNOU, R. (1), 'La Contemplation chez Plotin', in *Dictionnaire de spiritualité*, ii (Paris, 1950), 1729–38.

——(2), *Le Désir de Dieu dans la philosophie de Plotin* (Rome, 1967).

BALADI, N. (1), *La Pensée de Plotin* (Paris, 1970).

——(2), 'Origine et signification de l'audace chez Plotin', *Néoplatonisme*, 89–97.

BALTES, M., *Die Weltentstehung des Platonischen Timaios nach den antiken Interpreten*, i (Leiden, 1976).

BEIERWALTES, W. (1), *Platonismus und Idealismus* (Frankfurt, 1972.)

——(2), 'Reflexion und Einung: Zur Mystik Plotins', in W. Beierwaltes, H. von Balthasar, and A. Haas (eds.), *Grundfragen der Mystik* (Einsiedeln, 1974), 9–36.

——(3), *Marsilio Ficinos Theorie des Schönen im Kontext des Platonismus* (Heidelberg, 1980).

——(4), *Regio beatitudinis. Augustine's Concept of Happiness* (Villanova, 1981).

——(5), *Denken des Einen* (Frankfurt, 1985).

——(6), 'Plotins philosophische Mystik', in M. Schmidt and D. Bauer (eds.), *Grundfragen christlicher Mystik* (Stuttgart, 1987), 39–49.

——(7), 'Plotins Erbe', *Museum Helveticum*, 45 (1988), 75–97.

BLOIS, L. DE, *The Policy of the Emperor Gallienus* (Leiden, 1976).

BLUMENTHAL, H. (1), 'Did Plotinus Believe in Ideas of Individuals?', *Phronesis*, 11 (1966), 61–80.

——(2), *Plotinus' Psychology* (The Hague, 1971).

——(3), 'Soul, World-Soul, Individual Soul', *Néoplatonisme*, 56–63.

——(4), 'Nous and Soul in Plotinus: Some Problems of Demarcation', *Plotino*, 203–19.

——(5), 'Plotinus and Proclus on the Criterion of Truth', in P. Huby and G. Neal (eds.), *The Criterion of Truth* (Liverpool, 1989), 257–80.

BRISSON, L., *Le Même et l'autre dans la structure ontologique du Timée de Platon* (Paris, 1974).

——*et al.*, *Porphyre: La Vie de Plotin* (Paris, 1982).

BUSSANICH, J., *The One and Its Relation to Intellect in Plotinus* (Leiden, 1988).

The Cambridge Ancient History, xii: *The Imperial Crisis and Recovery A.D. 193–324* (Cambridge, 1939).

CHARRUE, J,. *Plotin lecteur de Platon* (Paris, 1978).

CHASTEL, A., *Marsile Ficin et l'art* (Geneva, 1954; 2nd edn. 1975).

CHERNISS, H. (1), *The Riddle of the Early Academy* (Berkeley, Calif., 1945).

——(2), 'The Sources of Evil According to Plato', in H. Cherniss, *Selected Papers*, ed. L. Tarán (Leiden, 1977), 253–60.

CORRIGAN, K., 'Body's Approach to Soul: An Examination of a Recurrent Theme in the Enneads', *Dionysius*, 9 (1985), 37–52.

COSTELLO, E., 'Is Plotinus Inconsistent on the Nature of Evil?', *International Philosophical Quarterly*, 7 (1967), 483–97.

DANIÉLOU, J., 'Plotin et Grégoire de Nysse sur le mal', *Plotino*, 485–94.

DECK, J., *Nature, Contemplation and the One: A Study in the Philosophy of Plotinus* (Toronto, 1967).

DILLON, J., *The Middle Platonists* (London, 1977).

DODDS, E. R. (1), 'The Parmenides of Plato and the Origin of the Neoplatonic "One" ', *Classical Quarterly*, 22 (1928), 129–43.

——(2), 'Tradition and Personal Achievement in the Philosophy of

Plotinus', _Journal of Roman Studies_, 50 (1960), 1–7 = Dodds, _The Ancient Concept of Progress and Other Essays_ (Oxford, 1973), essay VIII.

——(3), _Pagan and Christian in an Age of Anxiety_ (Cambridge, 1965).

DONINI, P., _Le scuole, l'anima, l'impero: La filosofia antica da Antioco a Plotino_ (Turin, 1982).

DÖRRIE, H., _Platonica minora_ (Munich, 1976).

ELSAS, C., _Neuplatonische und gnostische Weltablehnung in der Schule Plotins_ (Berlin, 1975).

EMILSSON, E. (1), _Plotinus on Sense-Perception: A Philosophical Study_ (Cambridge, 1988).

——(2), 'Reflections on Plotinus' _Ennead_ IV 2', in S. Teodorsson (ed.), _Greek and Latin Studies in Memory of Cajus Fabricius_ (Göteborg, 1990), 206–19.

——(3), 'Plotinus on the Objects of Thought' (forthcoming).

FERWERDA, R., _La Signification des images et des métaphores dans la pensée de Plotin_ (Groningen, 1965).

FESTUGIÈRE, A. J., _La Révélation d'Hermès Trismégiste_, 4 vols. (Paris, 1944–54).

FREDE, M., 'La teoría de las ideas de Longino', _Méthexis_, 3 (1990), 85–98.

FULLER, B., _The Problem of Evil in Plotinus_ (Cambridge, 1912).

GAISER, K., _Platons ungeschriebene Lehre_ (Stuttgart, 1968).

GOTTSCHALK, H., 'Aristotelian Philosophy in the Roman World from the Time of Cicero to the End of the Second Century A.D.', _ANRW_ II. xxxvi. 2: 1079–174.

GRAESER, A., _Plotinus and the Stoics_ (Leiden, 1972).

HADOT, I., 'La Vie et l'œuvre de Simplicius d'après les sources grecques et arabes', in I. Hadot (ed.), _Simplicius: Sa vie, son œuvre, sa survie_ (Berlin, 1987), 3–39.

HADOT, P. (1), 'Être, vie, pensée chez Plotin et avant Plotin', _Sources_, 107–41.

——(2), 'L'Apport du néoplatonisme à la philosophie de la nature en Occident', _Eranos Jahrbuch_, 37 (1968), 91–132.

——(3), _Plotin ou la simplicité du regard_ (2nd edn., Paris, 1973).

——(4), _Exercices spirituels et philosophie antique_ (2nd edn., Paris, 1987) = _Spiritual Exercises and Ancient Philosophy_, trans. M. Chase (Oxford, 1991).

——(5), 'L'Union de l'âme avec l'intellect divin dans l'expérience mystique plotinienne', in G. Boss and G. Seel (eds.), _Proclus et son influence_ (Zurich, 1987), 3–27.

HENRY, P. (1), _Plotin et l'occident_ (Louvain, 1934).

——(2), 'Plotinus' Place in the History of Thought', in S. MacKenna, *Plotinus: The Enneads* (3rd. edn., London, 1956), pp. xxxiii–li.

HIMMERICH, W., *Eudaimonia: Die Lehre des Plotin von der Selbstverwirklichung des Menschen* (Würzburg, 1959).

HORN, H.-J., 'Stoische Symmetrie und Theorie des Schönen in der Kaiserzeit', *ANRW* II. xxxvi. 3: 1455–71.

IGAL, J. (1), *La cronología de la Vida de Plotino de Porfirio* (Bilbao, 1972).

——(2), 'Aristoteles y la evolución de la antropología de Plotino', *Pensamiento*, 35 (1979), 315–46.

JERPHAGNON, L., 'Platonopolis, ou Plotin entre le siècle et le rêve', in *Néoplatonisme: Mélanges offerts à Jean Trouillard = Cahiers de Fontenay* (1981) (Fontenay, 1981), 215–47.

JONAS, H. (1), *The Gnostic Religion* (Boston, 1958).

——(2), 'The Soul in Gnosticism and Plotinus', *Le Néoplatonisme*, 45–53 (repr. Jonas, *Philosophical Essays* (Englewood Cliffs, NJ, 1974)).

KEYSER, E. DE, *La Signification de l'art dans les Ennéades de Plotin* (Louvain, 1955).

KREMER, K., '*Bonum est diffusivum sui*: Ein Beitrag zum Verhältnis von Neuplatonismus und Christentum', *ANRW* II. xxxvi. 2: 994–1032.

LLOYD, A. (1), 'Non-discursive Thought: An Enigma of Greek Philosophy', *Proceedings of the Aristotelian Society*, 70 (1969–70), 261–74.

——(2), 'Plotinus on the Genesis of Thought and Existence', *Oxford Studies in Ancient Philosophy*, 5 (1987), 155–86.

LONG, A. (1), *Hellenistic Philosophy* (London, 1974).

——(2), 'Soul and Body in Stoicism', *Phronesis*, 27 (1982), 34–57.

——and SEDLEY, D., *The Hellenistic Philosophers* (Cambridge, 1987).

MANSFELD, J., *Studies in Later Greek Philosophy and Gnosticism* (London, 1989).

MATTER, P., *Zum Einfluß des platonischen Timaios auf das Denken Plotins* (Winterthur, 1964).

MERLAN, P., *Monopsychism, Mysticism, Metaconsciousness* (The Hague, 1963).

MORAUX, P., *Der Aristotelismus bei den Griechen*, ii (Berlin, 1984).

MOREAU, J., 'Origine et expressions du beau suivant Plotin', in *Néoplatonisme: Mélanges offerts à Jean Trouillard = Cahiers de Fontenay* (Fontenay, 1981), 249–63.

MORTLEY, R. (1), 'Negative Theology and Abstraction in Plotinus', *American Journal of Philology*, 96 (1975), 363–77.

——(2), *From Word to Silence* (Bonn, 1986).

NUSSBAUM, M., and RORTY, A. eds., *Essays on Aristotle's* De anima (Oxford, 1992).

O'BRIEN, D. (1), 'Plotinus on Evil: A Study of Matter and the Soul in Plotinus' Conception of Human Evil', *Néoplatonisme*, 113–46.

—— (2), 'Le Volontaire et la nécessité: Réflexions sur la descente de l'âme dans la philosophie de Plotin', *Revue philosophique*, 167 (1977), 401–22.

—— (3), 'Plotinus and the Gnostics on the Generation of Matter', in H. Blumenthal and R. Markus (eds.), *Neoplatonism and Christian Thought: Essays in Honour of A. H. Armstrong* (London, 1981), 108–23.

—— (4), 'The Origin of Matter and the Origin of Evil in Plotinus' Criticism of Gnostics', in R. Brague and J.-F. Courtine (eds.), *Herméneutique et ontologie: Mélanges . . . P. Aubenque* (Paris, 1990), 181–202.

—— (5), *Plotinus on the Origin of Matter* (Naples, 1991).

O'DALY, G. (1), *Plotinus' Philosophy of the Self* (Shannon, 1973).

—— (2), 'The Presence of the One in Plotinus', *Plotino*, 159–69.

O'MEARA, D. (1), 'A propos d'un témoignage sur l'expérience mystique de Plotin (Enn. IV. 8 [6]. 1. 1–11)', *Mnemosyne*, 27 (1974), 238–44.

—— (2), *Structures hiérarchiques dans la pensée de Plotin* (Leiden, 1975).

—— (3), 'The Problem of Omnipresence in Plotinus *Ennead* VI. 4–5: A Reply', *Dionysius*, 4 (1980), 62–74.

—— (4), 'Gnosticism and the Making of the World in Plotinus', in B. Layton (ed.), *The Rediscovery of Gnosticism* (Leiden, 1980), i. 373–7.

—— (5), 'Plotinus on How Soul Acts on Body', in D. O'Meara (ed.), *Platonic Investigations* (Washington, DC, 1985), 247–62.

—— (6), 'Le Problème du discours sur l'indicible chez Plotin', *Revue de théologie et de philosophie*, 122 (1990), 145–56.

—— (7), 'Plotinus', in F. Cranz and P. Kristeller (eds.), *Catalogus translationum et commentariorum*, vol. vii (Washington, DC, 1992).

PANOFSKY, E., *Idea: A Concept in Art Theory*, Eng. trans. (New York, 1968).

PÉPIN, J. (1). 'Éléments pour une histoire de la relation entre l'intelligence et l'intelligible chez Platon et dans le néoplatonisme', *Revue philosophique*, 146 (1956), 39–55 = J. Pépin, *De la philosophie ancienne à la théologie patristique* (London, 1986), study i.

—— (2), 'Linguistique et théologie dans la tradition platonicienne', *Langages*, 65 (1982), 91–116.

QUISPEL, G., *Gnostic Studies* (Istanbul, 1974).

RÉMONDON, R., *La Crise de l'empire romain de Marc Aurèle à Anastase* (Paris, 1964).

RICH, A. (1), 'Reincarnation in Plotinus', *Mnemosyne*, 10 (1957), 232–8.

——(2), 'Plotinus and the Theory of Artistic Imitation', *Mnemosyne*, 13 (1960), 233–9.

——(3), 'Body and Soul in Plotinus', *Journal of the History of Philosophy*, 1 (1963), 2–15.

RICHARD, M., *L'Enseignement oral de Plotin* (Paris, 1986).

RIST, J. (1), 'Plotinus on Matter and Evil', *Phronesis*, 6 (1961), 154–66.

——(2), 'The Indefinite Dyad and Intelligible Matter in Plotinus', *Classical Quarterly*, 12 (1962), 99–107.

——(3), 'The Neoplatonic One and Plato's *Parmenides*', *Transactions of the American Philological Association*, 93 (1962), 389–401.

——(4), 'Forms of Individuals in Plotinus', *Classical Quarterly*, 13 (1963), 223–31.

——(5), 'Monism: Plotinus and Some Predecessors', *Harvard Studies in Classical Philology*, 69 (1965), 339–44.

——(6), *Plotinus: The Road to Reality* (Cambridge, 1967).

——(7), 'The One of Plotinus and the God of Aristotle', *Review of Metaphysics*, 27 (1973), 75–87 = Rist (10), study IX.

——(8), 'Plotinus and Augustine on Evil', *Plotino*, 495–508.

——(9), 'Metaphysics and Psychology in Plotinus' Treatment of the Soul', in L. Gerson (ed.), *Graceful Reason: Essays . . . Presented to Joseph Owens* (Toronto, 1983), 135–51 = Rist (10), study X.

——(10), *Platonism and Its Christian Heritage* (London, 1985).

ROBINSON, J. (ed.), *The Nag Hammadi Library in English* (New York, 1977).

RUDOLPH, K., *Gnosis: The Nature and History of Gnosticism* (Edinburgh, 1984; New York, 1987).

RUTTEN, C., *Les Catégories du monde sensible dans les Ennéades de Plotin* (Paris, 1961).

SANTA CRUZ DE PRUNES, M., *La Genèse du monde sensible dans la philosophie de Plotin* (Paris, 1979).

SCHROEDER, F. (1), 'Saying and Having in Plotinus', *Dionysius*, 9 (1985), 75–82.

——(2), 'Conversion and Consciousness in Plotinus, *Enneads* 5, 1 (10), 7'', *Hermes*, 114 (1986), 186–95.

——(3), 'Ammonius Saccas', *ANRW* II. xxxvi. 1: 493–526.

SCHWYZER, H.-R. (1), *Plotinos* (Munich, 1978) = G. Wissowa (ed.), *Paulys Realencyclopädie der classischen Altertumswissenschaft*, xxi. 1 (Stuttgart, 1951), 471–592, 1276, suppl. vol. xv (Munich, 1978), 311–28.

——(2), *Ammonios Sakkas der Lehrer Plotins* (Opladen, 1983).

SHARPLES, R., 'Alexander of Aphrodisias: Scholasticism and Innovation', *ANRW* II. xxxvi. 2: 1176–243.

STRAATEN, M. VAN, 'On Plotinus IV, 7[2], 8²', J. Mansfeld and L. de Rijk (eds.) *Kephalaion: Studies . . . Offered to C. J. de Vogel* (Assen, 1975), 164–70.

SZLEZÁK, T., *Platon und Aristoteles in der Nuslehre Plotins* (Basle, 1979).

TIGERSTEDT, E., *The Decline and Fall of the Neoplatonic Interpretation of Plato* (Helsinki, 1974).

TROUILLARD, J. (1), *La Purification plotinienne* (Paris, 1955).

——(2), *La Procession plotinienne* (Paris, 1955).

WALLIS, R. (1), *Neoplatonism* (London, 1972).

——(2), 'Scepticism and Neoplatonism', *ANRW* II, xxxvi. 2: 911–54.

WHITTAKER, J. (1), *Studies in Platonism and Patristic Thought* (London, 1984).

——(2), 'Platonic Philosophy in the Early Centuries of the Empire', *ANRW* II. xxxvi. 1: 81–123.

WURM, K., *Substanz und Qualität: Ein Beitrag zur Interpretation der plotinischen Traktate VI. 1. 2. und 3* (Berlin, 1973).

Index of Plotinian Texts

Index of Terms and Themes